MINDFULNESS
FOR WORRIERS

MINDFULNESS FOR WORRIERS

OVERCOME EVERYDAY STRESS AND ANXIETY

PADRAIG O'MORAIN

First published in Great Britain in 2015 by Yellow Kite
An imprint of Hodder & Stoughton
An Hachette UK company

1

Copyright © Padraig O'Morain 2015

The right of Padraig O'Morain to be identified as the Author
of the Work has been asserted by him in accordance with the
Copyright, Designs and Patents Act 1988.

A CIP catalogue record for this title is available from the British Library

ISBN 978 1 529 31258 4

Typeset in Bembo by Palimpsest Book Production Limited,
Falkirk, Stirlingshire
Printed and bound by Clays Ltd, St Ives plc

Hodder & Stoughton policy is to use papers that are natural,
renewable and recyclable products and made from wood grown in
sustainable forests. The logging and manufacturing processes are expected to
conform to the environmental regulations of the country of origin.

Hodder & Stoughton Ltd
Carmelite House
50 Victoria Embankment
London
EC4Y 0DZ

www.hodder.co.uk

To my father, Arthur Morrin, and my mother, Lil Murphy

ABOUT THE AUTHOR

Padraig O'Morain is a writer and psychotherapist. He has practised mindfulness for a quarter of a century. During that time, he has trained a wide variety of people in mindfulness – from accountants to search and rescue crew – in both Ireland and the UK, and throughout the world online. He writes a weekly column for the *Irish Times* and his books include *Mindfulness on the Go: Peace in Your Pocket, Light Mind: Mindfulness for Daily Living* and a poetry collection, *The Blue Guitar*. He lives in Dublin with his wife and two daughters.

CONTENTS

PART TWO: TURNING DOWN THE VOLUME OF OUR THOUGHTS

PART THREE: STOPPING THE WORRY SPIRAL

PART FIVE: GETTING IT
RIGHT OR GETTING STUCK?

PART SIX: THE STRESS EFFECT:
OUR BODIES AND OTHER BODIES

PART SEVEN: A NEW RELATIONSHIP WITH WORRY, STRESS AND ANXIETY

HOW TO USE THIS BOOK

You can read this book straight through or dip in whenever you wish. The Introduction is worth reading first though, and if you're not familiar with mindfulness, read Mindfulness: The Basics.

At the end of each chapter you will find two suggested practices related to the theme of that chapter.

Scattered throughout the book are more practices and ideas for you to try out.

If you go to www.padraigomorain.com/audios, you will find a collection of short talks and practices related to this book, which are free to download.

INTRODUCTION

This book is about dropping worry, which means that it is also about changing your relationship with anxiety and stress, as the three are closely related.

Think of anxiety as a source of stress.

Think of worry as the agent that amplifies that stress.

I cannot help you get rid of anxiety and stress. This is vital to understand. Anxiety and stress are an inescapable aspect of the human condition and of living in an unpredictable world. A level of anxiety is inevitable in life.

But I can help you learn to drop the kind of thinking – worrying – that generates unnecessary, extra levels of stress. This can bring enormous relief, as you can lighten the load a little and clear some space in your mind.

WHAT IS ANXIETY?

Anxiety is fear about possibilities in the future or unknown possibilities in the present.

I

It is fear of the future: *Will I lose my job when the company is downsizing next month?*

And it is fear of an unknown present possibility: *What is in that envelope I have just been handed by my manager?*

WHAT IS STRESS?

Stress is a series of physical events caused by anxiety. These events include increases in adrenalin and cortisol in your system, faster heart rate, faster breath, physical tension, and increases in the production of glucocorticoids, which can cause ulcers.

WHAT IS WORRY?

Worry is rumination. It is going over and over possibilities for the future in a way that is based on fear. We can worry about the past, too – *What did they say about me when I did that?* – and the present – *I'm late, this is terrible.*

Worry, anxiety and stress can all amplify each other. The inevitable level of anxiety that attaches to many situations can be increased by worry, which then also increases stress, which again also increases anxiety. It can be a vicious circle.

Happily, we can reduce or eliminate the unnecessary, self-generated stress and anxiety by stepping out of the habit of **worrying**.

Worry is a waste of energy and serves no purpose. For

instance, if you are on the way to an appointment for which you suspect you will be late, you are likely to feel anxiety, assuming the appointment matters to you. But most of that anxiety will be from self-generated thoughts that you are turning over in your mind as you hurry along. Thoughts such as, *'This is terrible, I'm going to be late. What if she doesn't wait for me? What will they think about me?'* – in other words, worry. These thoughts are unhelpful and make you feel worse. In this book, I am going to show you how mindfulness can help you step out of the loop of exaggerated thoughts and end the cycle of worry. You will learn to accept and live with a certain level of anxiety, but no longer will your mind be crippled by worrying thoughts.

'HELPFUL' AND 'EXAGGERATED' ANXIETY

Often (though not always), anxiety energises us. I have many items on my to-do list – especially keeping my accounts in order – that I would never get around to unless a little anxiety about the consequences of ignoring them prodded me into devoting time and energy to them. Similarly, although I don't find exercise terribly enjoyable, a little thread of anxiety about what will happen to me if I let myself go helps me to get down to it first thing in the day.

So anxiety helps to get things done that wouldn't otherwise get done. However, exaggerated anxiety (in other words, the extra anxiety that worry piles on top of the anxiety that's already there) might frighten me off getting started on the book-keeping or the exercise.

When I said that anxiety motivates us, I added in brackets 'though not always'. If I am waiting on the outcome of an important interview about a promotion, and I badly need the money that would go with the promotion, then I am likely to experience anxiety. However, in this case the anxiety doesn't help to motivate me because there isn't really anything I can do except wait. The anxiety isn't motivating me into useful action, it's just there.

But by mindfully accepting this anxiety without thinking my way into the exaggerated variety that spirals out of control, I can get through this waiting period in good shape. I might or might not use the energy of the basic anxiety to encourage me to clean the house or to go for long walks, and that's fine. But whatever I choose to do, I need to let the basic anxiety run its course without turning it into something worse in my mind. If I can accept the anxiety, then I can stop it from spiralling.

CREATING EXAGGERATED ANXIETY

So how do we create exaggerated anxiety, and how do we strip it away so that we only have basic anxiety to deal with? Getting the hang of this is fundamental in terms of managing anxiety and worry.

Awfulising

We create exaggerated anxiety by telling ourselves how awful it will be if such a thing happens or doesn't happen, and by dramatising it in what are, frankly, silly ways. *'If I don't get that promotion I will be ruined, I will be hauled off to a debtors' prison, people will laugh at me, I will be on the front pages of the newspapers*, DID NOT GET PROMOTION SHOCK. *Even my ancestors will shake their heads with disappointment.'* That's awfulising.

Physical escalation

We can also engage in physical behaviour that ramps up our anxiety levels. I'm driving along, late for that appointment. I hunch over and grab the steering wheel. I put my foot down, even though I am on a road with frequent traffic lights for which I will have to stop anyway. I curse at other drivers. I double-curse when the light turns red. I punch the steering wheel, sorely tempting the airbag to explode.

We can drop the worries that are behind these behaviours through the practice of mindfulness. Mindfulness is an extremely helpful tool when it comes to overcoming exaggerated anxiety, including awfulising and the escalation of physical tension that goes with it.

TRY THESE

These two techniques can be especially beneficial in preventing helpful anxiety from spiralling into exaggerated anxiety.

Step out of the story and come to your breath. Learn to redirect your attention. If your attention is on the scary story in your mind, then you risk getting lost in exaggerated anxiety. If, instead, you turn your attention to the simple act of breathing, then the exaggerated anxiety will fade. It is important, though, that you do not simply transfer the agitation to your breathing – in other words, breathe as slowly and as normally as you can; gulping the breath can only make matters worse.

Instead of stressing your body, observe it. Remember the physical exaggeration I mentioned before – punching the steering wheel, driving too fast and so on? You will probably find that as soon as you notice this happening, and bring your awareness to your body and how it is reacting to the situation, you will tend to stop doing it. Why? Because deep down you know it is nothing but a waste of time that will get you nowhere and could even potentially harm you. So, in this case, notice what your hands feel like on the steering wheel, notice how your back feels against the seat and notice how your chest and tummy move while you breathe. Of course, if you are doing this in your car you need to give most of your attention to the road, but maintaining a calm background awareness of your body will help you avoid losing control of your emotions and stressing out unnecessarily.

Dodge the second arrow: This is an idea based on the Buddhist metaphor of the two arrows. If you are hit by an arrow, the story goes, you will experience pain. The pain is inevitable. Nothing, including mindfulness practice, can prevent it. But if you react by exaggerating your pain, by revisiting it in your mind again and again long after it has died down, then you have shot a second arrow into yourself. In mindfulness, we work with that second arrow. By practising the mindfulness exercises I outline in this book, you will learn to return to awareness of your breath, your body or your activities whenever you notice yourself slipping into unhelpful ruminations – i.e. the second arrow – about the past or exaggerations about the future.

For instance, if you have an important exam coming up, that naturally brings a certain anxiety with it and that's the first arrow. But by continually turning those anxious thoughts over in your mind – *Oh My God, what if I can't answer any of the questions? What if I fail?* – you are firing a second arrow. When you notice that second arrow, and the feelings and physical tensions that go with it, mindfully return to your preparations for the exam or to your breath or to that cup of tea you are drinking right now.

Every life has its stresses, anxieties and worries. They cannot be avoided. But mindfulness will help you keep the pain of these stresses, anxieties and worries to a minimum. It is an extremely powerful tool that you can keep with you at all times, and use whenever you need it. If you are a 'worrier', learning mindfulness will greatly improve your experience of life.

PART ONE: ALL ABOUT MINDFULNESS

MINDFULNESS – THE BASICS

It's likely that you will have heard the term 'mindfulness'. In recent times, it's been mentioned more and more on TV and radio and in newspapers – and that's because Westerners have realised the powerful potential of this simple practice, which has its origins in Eastern tradition. What follows here is a brief but useful introduction to the basics of mindfulness, for – as I said above – those who haven't encountered the term before or those who have, but would like a recap.

WHAT IS MINDFULNESS?

In a nutshell, mindfulness is returning your attention, with acceptance, from your thoughts to your experience in this moment.

What is meant by 'your experience in this moment'?

It means whatever you are doing or noticing right now. Examples could include:

- Your breathing

- What you see

- Your movement as you walk or reach

- Your physical feelings

- What you hear, smell, taste or touch

What is acceptance?

Acceptance means being aware of your experience without immediately commenting on it, analysing it, or criticising it. It isn't surrender and it isn't resignation. It is allowing yourself to 'take in' the experience as it is for a few moments.

What is the point of acceptance?

Our reactions to experiences and and feelings are often habitual and unhelpful. When we bring mindful acceptance to a situation, and to the feelings we have about it, we can take a fresh look; we are no longer driven by these habitual reactions, and very often we can see new and more useful choices. I include feelings here because sometimes it is our own feelings that we find hard to accept – for instance, feelings of anxiety.

And what is the point of returning your attention?

In order to do what I have described, you have to be aware, and in the moment. Otherwise you could be going around in a bit of a trance.

What do you mean, a 'trance'?

I mean paying more attention to what's going on inside your head than to what is happening in reality outside it.

What's wrong with that?

It means you get caught up easily in worries, anxiety, resentments or regrets instead of dealing with reality. Very often, what's going on in your head is far more distressing than what's happening in your immediate, real world. It's far better to return your attention, with acceptance, to your experience in this moment.

What are some ways of doing this?

Notice your breathing. You might notice the breath against your nostrils, or your chest gently rising and falling. Move your attention from your thoughts to the sensations in your feet. Quietly observe what your body feels like. Listen to sounds in your vicinity, but without judging them just for the moment. When you are walking around, either inside or outside, pay attention to the experience of walking.

Do I have to go around doing this all day?

No, these are just ways of bringing your attention back when it drifts, which it will, a lot. They help you to build up the skill of being mindful.

Do I have to meditate in the lotus position?

No. You might see mindfulness illustrated that way on the Internet and in magazines, but most people who practise mindfulness are unable to do it in that way though I have lots of admiration for people who can. Most people who practise mindfulness do so while going about their everyday business – walking to work, drinking a cup of tea, cooking or washing up, etc.

What if I don't have the time to spend ages concentrating on my breath?

There are two ways to do mindfulness. Meditating mindfully for long periods of time is one; the other is to build mindfulness into your day with practices that are short and simple. The latter is the method you will learn in this book.

But don't we have to think all the time?

No. Your thoughts can often be useful or entertaining, but more often than you might imagine they can be useless or stressful or just plain wrong. And spending your time going over and over negative thoughts in your head can trip you into depression. So sometimes it's good *not* to think!

HOW DO YOU BREATHE?

Practice: Notice what your breathing is like: fast, slow; deep, shallow; rough, smooth; tight, free.

Commentary: Why do you breathe the way you do right now? Many reasons: your breathing may be affected by what's happening to you at the moment; it may be affected by what you're thinking about – worry can 'tighten' your breathing, for instance. Your habitual breathing style could have been influenced by your parents or by the emotions they most often expressed. Checking the quality of your breathing is a powerful way to become aware of these influences and to respond to what's really happening right now.

Tips: When you check in with how you are breathing, see if you can connect it with your current emotions or with your way of facing the world. A person who mostly faces the world with calm will breathe differently to someone who mostly brings anxiety to his or her relationship with the world. Watch how your breath changes as you observe it.

SLOW BODY SCAN

Practice: Move your awareness slowly up your body from your toes to the top of your head. When worries intrude, return to wherever you are in the scan.

Commentary: The body scan calms the emotions as well as the body. The act of moving your awareness from your toes to the top of your head can bring about that state of calm surprisingly effectively. Move your awareness from your toes through your legs up through your body and arms to the very top of your head. I would suggest doing this for no more than 20 minutes, but 5–10 minutes is fine. If you feel anxiety instead of calm, gently stop doing the scan.

Tips: As you do the body scan, your worries and preoccupations will cross your mind. When you notice them, quietly return your attention to your body. If worries keep you from sleeping at night, try the body scan, repeating it if necessary. You have a good chance of drifting off to sleep at some stage during the scan.

RETURN. INVITE SILENCE: A MINDFULNESS FORMULA

Once, at the end of a workshop, a lady came up to me and complained that the whole idea of 'being in the now' meant nothing to her. What's the 'now' anyway, she asked? I had to confess that I was not quite sure what the 'now' was. It might be the moment you're in but, as I explained to the lady, by the time you realise you are 'in the moment', that moment has gone into the past. It was because of that difficulty in working out what the 'now' was that I looked for another way of describing mindfulness practice.

MINDFULNESS IN ALL SITUATIONS

What we need is a method to bring us into mindfulness in all situations and especially when we're feeling anxious. Here's a two-part formula that will help you to do that. It sidesteps the not very helpful argument about the 'now', what it is and whether it exists at all:

Return.

Invite silence.

Let's look at what this means.

Return

Returning means returning your attention from your imagination or thoughts. But return to what? You return to the anchor point. We all know that an anchor keeps a boat from drifting away. If the boat begins to drift, then the anchor pulls it back. We can develop a mindfulness anchor to stop us from drifting too far into the stories and worries in our mind. That anchor then helps us to return when we get lost in our own minds.

What is that anchor? For most people, it can be the breath. But more precisely, it's the breath at a particular spot. So it might be just that point where the breath enters your nostrils. It might be the feeling of the breath inside your nostrils. It might be the back of your throat, your chest, your stomach, the area between chest and stomach, your back . . . any could serve as the anchor, and which you prefer is really a matter of personal choice.

To find out where the anchor is, or to experiment with deciding where it should be, observe your breathing quietly for a little while. Ask yourself where in your body you are most aware of the breath. It's probably going to be in one of the places mentioned above. For me, it's at the entrance to my nostrils.

What you need to do now is establish that anchor point as an object of mindfulness. By an 'object of mindfulness', I mean something you bring your attention to when you want to be mindful. So now and then, spend some minutes observing your breath at that anchor point. This is how you establish the anchor point. Then, whenever you want to get into the 'mindfulness zone', use that point as your anchor. It takes only a little practice to do this.

Why a specific anchor point? If you asked an archer to shoot an arrow into a forest, she might ask you which tree you want her to hit. From the archer's point of view, everything works more smoothly if she has a target. Now she knows where to direct her aim, her skill and her effort.

So what you're really doing in establishing the anchor is choosing a target for your mindfulness.

The more you practise returning to the anchor point, the better you become at quickly moving into mindfulness. That in turn means that you can bring yourself quickly into an enjoyment of the benefits of mindfulness.

You can go to the anchor point at any time. For instance, if you tend to wake up and worry during the night, you can move out of your worries by moving into awareness of the anchor point. If you're in a business meeting and you're feeling stressed, you can move from your stressful thoughts and straight to awareness of the anchor point.

But it's not only a matter of having an anchor point, of how you return to an awareness of the present moment.

Awareness on its own isn't mindfulness. Awareness plus *acceptance* is mindfulness. So that brings us to:

Invite silence

What is acceptance? It isn't agreement, or surrender or resignation. It is allowing things to be as they are for a time, to allow yourself to experience the reality of the situation. You do so without commenting on it in your head. In other words, you invite a little silence into your mind during that time.

So if my computer crashes and I haven't saved an important document, I gain nothing by flinging the computer or myself around the room. Instead, I can come to my anchor point. Then, instead of making speeches inside my head about my stupidity, I can introduce a few moments of silence to my mind. In those few moments, I have an opportunity to experience the situation without burning energy in condemnation and criticism. In other words, I know that the computer has crashed and that the document is lost and that is enough. I switch the computer back on and I check around to see if the document might have been saved, at least partially, somewhere accessible. Whatever the outcome, I have spared myself the extra upset I would have experienced had I lost myself in that storm of anger and condemnation. That doesn't mean I'm going to be completely stress-free at the prospect of writing the document again, it simply means that I keep my stress to the minimum.

So acceptance introduces some moments of silence in my head while I take in the situation and work out what needs to be done next. Similarly, if I notice that I feel happy, I could introduce some moments of silence and allow myself to enjoy the feeling. I don't need to analyse it away – I can simply accept it.

TRY THESE

Here are two ways to help you remember to apply the 'Return. Invite silence' formula, no matter how dire the situation.

Hit 'return'. When you write on a computer, you hit the return key to get to a new paragraph. See if you can visualise 'hitting the return key' to remind you to return to awareness of your anchor point. At the start, you'll have to slow down before you hit return in order to remember to be mindful at the same time. In time, though, it will become more natural. You won't always remember to do it but you will remember often enough. When you return, invite silence into your mind for a few moments. Again, you won't always have time for this, but try it – you might like it.

Practise in stress-free situations. The more you practise mindfulness in simple, stress-free situations, the more easily you will be able to move into mindfulness when you are anxious or worried. So when you're shopping or when you have a pause at work, try the 'Return. Invite silence' formula. Also try it when you are in a pleasant location, perhaps in a park or garden, and it will enhance your enjoyment.

◯ QUICK THOUGHT: Practise the formula 'Return. Invite silence' to bring yourself to mindful acceptance in any situation.

GIVE 5 PER CENT

Practice: Give 5 per cent of your attention to your breathing as you carry out simple tasks, walk or watch TV.

Commentary: Giving 5 per cent of your attention to your breathing can increase your awareness of what is going on in the moment by anchoring you to the here and now. Distraction – including distraction in the form of worries – will set in, but returning to that 5 per cent will help you cultivate presence of mind in all sorts of everyday situations. Don't get anxious about measuring the 5 per cent. I am really talking about keeping a thread of awareness on your breathing.

Tips: Deliberately set out to do a series of office or household tasks while keeping that thread of awareness on your breathing. Whenever unhelpful worries enter your mind, return to that thread. Now and then, sit and do nothing except maintain awareness of the thread of breathing.

BUSY MINDS: PUTTING THOUGHTS IN THEIR PLACE

When I lived in a bedsitter (a one-room apartment) in Dublin many years ago, a woman called Joan moved into the bedsitter above mine. When Joan walked around her room, I could hear her footsteps on my ceiling. On the evening she moved in, the footsteps went on for hours. Fair enough, I thought, she is busy unpacking and arranging her stuff in the room. But the footsteps went on evening after evening. Every night I fell asleep to the sound of her footsteps.

What could be going on? I got an inkling after meeting Joan a couple of times in the hallway and seeing that she was so preoccupied she scarcely noticed I was there. She seemed to have a permanent furrow in her forehead from endless thinking. But Joan wasn't just thinking, she was over-thinking. She had a busy, busy mind.

Eventually, I stopped noticing Joan's footsteps because of that human capacity we have that enables us to get used to anything. But I sometimes wonder where Joan is today.

Is she still caught up in her endless thinking? Is she still wearing a track in the carpet wherever she lives, as she walks around and around with that furrowed brow? I hope she's escaped from all that, because it was pretty clear to me that she wasn't finding any peace or answers in her thinking, and her thinking was, in fact, cutting her off from the real world.

THINKING: HOW VALUABLE IS IT?

Because we are so given, in our era, to putting the mind and the brain above all else, we can very easily make a fundamental mistake: this is to assume that thinking is always a valuable and necessary action in itself. Suppose I were to ask you to wave your arms about instead of thinking – you would quickly decide that this was a pretty silly waste of time. But really, a lot of the thinking we do is no less silly. And that's especially true if, like Joan, you have a very busy mind.

We have a habit of treating our thoughts as though they are a whole experience, but really our thoughts are just one aspect of our experience. People who practise mindfulness spend less time thinking and worrying – and when they find themselves lost in thought, they bring themselves back into awareness. But doesn't this prevent them from solving problems? On the contrary, very often they discover that solutions to problems, and other creative ideas, arise more easily. This is because the brain often works out solutions at a subconscious level. When you stop all of that over-thinking, the solutions have an opportunity to get through into your awareness.

Indeed, when you practise mindfulness you will more often experience that 'eureka' moment many of us have when we stop thinking about a task. The solution suddenly appears, as if from nowhere, while we're engaged in a totally different activity.

'Lose your mind and come to your senses' was the advice given by the mindfulness teacher Anthony de Mello S.J. It's good advice. It means giving more atten-tion to awareness of your body and of what's going on for you physically than to the thoughts in your head. This is not an anti-thinking approach. It is about seeing thinking as being valuable in its place and time but not something that needs to occupy every place and every time.

In mindfulness, we give our thoughts less importance. We know that while our thoughts can be useful, they can also be deceptive and unhelpful. One of the benefits of practising mindfulness is that your thoughts begin to take their proper place in your life. They become the servant and not the master.

TRY THESE

Here are two ways in which you can use your mindfulness practice to quieten an over-busy mind.

Accept uncertainty. One of the core ideas behind mindfulness is that everything is impermanent. As the old Buddhist texts put it: 'Everything arises, everything passes.' This is not something to fight but something to accept. We begin to get some peace of mind when we accept that everything is impermanent and that therefore uncertainty is built into the system. No matter how much thinking you do, the solutions you arrive at are impermanent and could stop working at any time. All the more reason to accept that a search for the perfect solution is fruitless. Learn to relax a little and be satisfied instead with a 'good enough' solution that you can adjust later on in accordance with circumstances. There's more on this in the chapter called 'Always in beta: Lifting the curse of perfectionism' (see page 125).

Get to know your body. Now and then, stand still, with your arms by your sides. Take your attention out of your mind and put it on your body. Imagine that you're standing beneath a shower and that the water is your awareness. The awareness moves from the top of your head right down to your feet. Can you now spend a minute without being diverted into a series of thoughts about whatever your main preoccupation is at the moment? As you stand, adjust your balance as necessary and notice the adjustment. You'll find that many such adjustments are going on all the time. Notice what your feet feel like against the floor. Notice how your arms feel beside your body. Every time your mind tells you it has more important things to do, namely thinking, gently bring your attention back to your body.

○ QUICK THOUGHT: Practise awareness of your body, and accept uncertainty, to help free you from the tyranny of an overactive mind.

'NO PROBLEM-SOLVING' BREAKS

Practice: Take brief periods during which you promise yourself you will make no attempt whatsoever to solve any of your problems.

Commentary: Do you mull over problems in your head when you go for a walk or drive or lie in bed awake at night? If so, you're normal. But endless problem-solving isn't necessary or helpful, and much of it falls into the category of pointless worry. To give yourself a break from this, drop your problem-solving efforts during certain periods, such as mealtimes, that were never designed for problem-solving.

Tips: Next time you plan to walk, eat, drive or go to bed, decide all your problems will still be exactly the same when you finish as they were before you began. When you slip into problem-solving mode, as you will, silently say 'not now' and bring your attention back to the activity you're undertaking. Letting your mind take a rest like this will allow your subconscious to play with the problem in the meantime and perhaps even to suggest a solution when you return to it.

PART TWO: TURNING DOWN THE VOLUME OF OUR THOUGHTS

JUST WORRYING: DON'T AMPLIFY WORRY

Julie starts to worry. Did she actually send that email last night containing a key piece of information for colleagues who will meet a prospective customer this morning? She remembers that she put the information together. She remembers that she opened her email program. But did she send it? The more she thinks about it, the more agitated and uncomfortable she feels.

Right now, Julie is on a train to meet another customer in another part of the country. The Wi-Fi on the train is terribly bad and so is the connectivity on her phone. It could be an hour before she can check that she sent that email. By then, her colleagues will already be at the meeting. She knows she sent them a great deal of information yesterday evening. But this particular piece of information?

She goes over and over it all in her mind, as the countryside flashes past. She imagines the consequences for her colleagues – how will they secure the contract without this vital information? An hour later, the signal improves and she quickly goes online to find that she had, of course, sent the email.

But even if she found that she had not sent the email, that would not have been the real problem as she sat there hunched up and worrying for an hour. Why? Because the email itself is not the real problem. The real problem is that Julie finds it difficult to tolerate uncertainty and worry. As a result, she makes the effects of worry far worse than they need to be.

That's what people who 'over-worry' do – they take the worry they already have and they amplify it.

TURNING DOWN THE VOLUME OF WORRY

Mindfulness could provide Julie with an alternative to amplifying her worries and could make a huge difference to her experience of life. Over time, she would have fewer negative reactions to situations and the reactions she had would be less strong – that's an effect mindfulness has been found to have. She would no longer be so quick to get lost in a spiral of worrying over the possibility that something might have gone wrong. She would be more aware of her own reactions and this would enable her to begin to implement mindfulness techniques. She would even relax on that train and not complain that the countryside was flashing by too slowly.

Am I saying she would never worry again if she was mindful? Not at all, but she would understand that worries will come into her head whether she likes it or not. She would understand that her job is to ensure that she doesn't amplify these worries by 'catastrophising' them. Whenever we feel a mismatch between how we want things to be and how we fear they will turn out, worry and anxiety move in to fill that gap. If Julie lets this carry her away, then she will become lost in a forest of worry.

The first thing Julie needs to do when worries come into her head is to accept their presence without over-reacting to them. She needs to see that she is 'just worrying'. If she can reduce her thoughts to this simple level, she won't get tangled up in anxiety just because she might have forgotten to send an email.

Mindfulness practice will encourage her to move from the worrying in her head to an awareness of her present experience in the real world. What's that experience? Perhaps it is the cup of coffee she is drinking or the music she is listening to. If she practises mindfulness when she is not worrying, she will find it easier to make that shift when she has something to worry about.

The mindfulness muscle: The point of practising mind-fulness of drinking your tea or of your breathing or of walking is to build your 'mindfulness muscle' to help you respond better later when specific issues, such as worry, make themselves felt. Mindfulness cultivated in all these easy, everyday ways – awareness of brushing your teeth, for instance – will change your response to the bigger issues. It's rather like doing stretches a couple of times a day to keep yourself supple for the entire day.

So that's the first step for Julie – to be able to move her focus from worry on to whatever she can do in the present moment. Perhaps she can see with more clarity what to do next. If that's not clear yet, perhaps she can drink her coffee in peace.

Note that we are not talking here about blocking out worries altogether but, rather, acknowledging their existence without being harmed by them. To shut our eyes and ears to reality – to ignore reality – is not part of mindfulness practice.

TRY THESE

Here are two ways to remind yourself to apply a mindful attitude when you're in a state of over-worrying.

Say 'just worrying'. Whenever you notice you are worrying, silently say 'just worrying' and return to what you're doing. What you are doing may well be taking action on the issue that is a source of worry – and that action may be getting blocked by your worrying. Or maybe, like Julie on the train, you are not in a position to take action. In that case, what you're doing may be talking to a friend or tackling another piece of work and worrying may be interfering with this, too. Moreover, the worrying itself probably contributes nothing to what's going on except to make you feel bad. But even if a certain background level of worry remains, that simple phrase 'just worrying' can help you to avoid magnifying it and letting it take over.

Do something you enjoy doing. To sit there repeating 'just worrying', 'just worrying', 'just worrying' is not really a very satisfactory way to spend your time. It's usually easier to put your attention to something that you value and enjoy. For some people that might be cooking, for others it might be going for a run, reading a book or playing with a child. Use that activity as your focus of mindfulness. This may require an effort at the start – your mind may protest that it would prefer to worry – but if you persist you will see the benefits. And you will find you have more energy to deal with the issue you had been worrying about.

Finally, remember that we can't get rid of worry altogether: it comes with the territory of life. But we can drop the habit of worrying we can make it something we do some of the time but not all of the time. Using the methods outlined above helps us to change our relationship with worry for the better.

◯ QUICK THOUGHT: When you notice you have begun to worry, silently say 'just worrying' and then get on with what you're doing or make a rational plan to deal with the issue you're worrying about.

CALMING THE LAKE

Practice: Imagine a lake that reflects your feelings and observe the lake until the water and your feelings are both calm.

Commentary: If you are a visual person in your thinking and learning style, this will be a really helpful way to calm your emotions. You need to give it a few minutes while you relax and imagine a lake and its surrounding trees and perhaps the sky. Breathing calmly, observe the lake and continue to do so until both you and the lake are calm. Remember that what you work with are your thoughts and your breathing. If you just pull back gently from thinking agitated thoughts and breathe calmly, your feelings are likely to follow.

Tips: When you are not feeling agitated but can put a little time aside, visualise the lake, the surrounding countryside and the sky above it. Identify the features that will reflect your feelings (the sky, the trees, the water, a small boat perhaps). Then, when you are actually agitated, you will already know where to go in your visualisation.

DOGS OF WORRY: DROP
IMAGINARY WORRIES

Jane submitted an assignment to her lecturer last week. Yesterday she looked back at the assignment, and noticed to her dismay that she had left spelling and grammatical errors in the conclusion. She had spotted these before submission but somehow the changes had not been saved.

An annoying and embarrassing occurrence without doubt. But Jane makes the experience worse by imagining her lecturer glaring at the mistakes, reaching for his giant red pen and marking her down. Will her lecturer see her for ever more as a careless student or, worse, a student whose command of spelling, grammar and syntax is really bad? Will she have to be extra careful in all future assignments because her lecturer will expect more mistakes?

Jane is multiplying her worries in ways that make no sense but are so common to so many of us. This brings me to the Dogs of Worry . . .

Imagine you are walking through a forest on your own.

Suddenly a large, angry-looking dog appears in your path, baring his teeth.

You tell yourself how awful this is but it's not over yet: another dog has appeared beside the first one. And this one looks every bit as unfriendly.

This isn't just awful – it's a catastrophe, you think. Suddenly two more dogs appear.

How unfair this is. All you wanted to do was to walk through the forest to relax and now you are confronted by these four scary dogs. Oh, and they've been joined by another four, so now you have eight scary dogs to contend with.

Suppose that seven of those eight dogs have been conjured up by your imagination. Suppose that only one dog exists, and that's the only one you need to pay attention to. The problem is, you've reacted to eight dogs, not one. And you may not even have focused your attention on the real dog.

That's how it is when the mind leaps to add memories, fantasies, fears and assumptions to our reality. Suddenly, challenges can seem many times worse than they really are and we can easily lose touch with the facts of our situation.

FOCUS ON THE ONE DOG

When we practise mindfulness, we return our attention to reality – to that one dog – when we find we have drifted away from what's actually happening. This helps us to negotiate our way through life with less fuss, less stress and fewer complications than would otherwise be the case. Oh, and with fewer dogs.

The method is as simple as moving our attention back to our breath, our walking, our posture, or to whatever else is going on now. The trick lies in being willing to bring our attention back, and in doing so often. If we do that, we will become skilled at reducing the number of dogs from eight to one.

It's easy for this sort of sequence of imaginary events to happen, especially when we see ourselves as up against a threat. Because our mind so often works by association, the discovery of the mistake may even link emotionally all the way back to childhood. For instance, you may have been criticised for childhood mistakes and these criticisms may have stayed with you. Then, even if the mistake you make isn't particularly significant, it can arouse old emotions that lead you to exaggerate their importance.

If Jane stopped worrying, she might remember that the rest of her assignment was well written and didn't contain errors. The lecturer would probably take this into account. In fact, Jane could even write an email to the lecturer and explain what had happened. That may help demonstrate that she is a diligent student but just made a mistake.

But her worrying stops her from seeing these possibilities and so she ends up in a ball of tension, caught in a scary fantasy about the lecturer's response. In other words, Jane has taken one dog and turned it into at least eight slavering hounds ready to pounce on her.

Because mindfulness discourages us from getting lost in grim imaginings, it makes it far less likely that we will multiply those dogs of worry. When we spot the process going on, we pull away by returning to awareness of the moment.

Note that mindfulness does not deny reality. That's a dog on the path, for sure; but it's only one dog. Mindfulness encourages us to focus on what 'is' rather than on conjuring up fantasies, and makes us far more skilful in working with reality. Jane's story underlines how mindfulness can help with planning. Planning is different to fantasy. If Jane needs to plan what to do about the issue of the mistakes in the assignment, that is quite different to sitting there lost in a fantasy about how terrible it is that she made mistakes. Fantasising generally gets nothing done; returning your attention to calmly working out your options allows you to make choices. Note, too, that while fantasy involves emotions, so does planning, but fewer of them. When planning, we may feel a certain tension, or a sense of anticipation, or one of a whole range of other emotions; but instead of letting them send us off into fantasy, we return to our plans.

TRY THESE

Here are two practices you can bring to bear when you find yourself staring at a huge pack of snarling imaginary dogs.

Ask, 'how true is this?'. When you find yourself lost in a scary scenario in your mind, you can ask yourself how true this mental drama is. To what extent are you dramatising the situation because our human tendency is to exaggerate negative emotions? Could it be that it's all less serious than you have told yourself? That it's one dog, not eight?

Spot the drama. When you notice yourself getting lost in an anxiety drama like this one, you can silently say 'drama' or even 'thinking'. Then return to whatever is going on in the present moment. That could include planning or it could include having a cup of coffee. The key is not to allow worries to increase and multiply, buzzing around you like wasps. Banish those wasps by using that label 'thinking' or 'drama' and return to your breathing, your walking, or awareness of your posture.

○ QUICK THOUGHT: Return your awareness to the issue at hand – one dog – instead of conjuring multitudes of problems – many dogs – in your imagination.

43

LET THE SECOND ARROW FALL

Practice: Accepting that a certain level of stress and anxiety is inevitable, focus on stepping back from the worries that make experiences worse than they need to be.

Commentary: An old Buddhist story tells us that to be struck by an arrow is inevitably painful. But if we dwell on what has happened, beyond the point at which thinking or talking about it is useful, then we are sticking a second arrow into ourselves. Life – even a day, sometimes – has many 'first arrows'. It's how we respond to these 'first arrows' that determines whether we add unnecessarily to our own suffering. The 'second arrow' is made up of thoughts, imaginings, memories and physical tensing. Using mindfulness to step back from these reactions can be thought of as 'letting the second arrow fall'.

Tips: When you find yourself getting carried away in your mind by your thoughts about the painful experience, acknowledge the presence of those thoughts and then gently move your attention to your breath. If you prefer, move your attention to your feet. If it helps, silently repeat the phrase, 'letting the second arrow fall'. (For more, see page 7.)

CRAZY THINKING: STEP DOWN FROM EXAGGERATION

'This is terrible!' I told myself one day when I wanted to do some business at an official office, only to find that it had been moved out of town. My business would have to wait until the following week. Awful. Then I remembered something: one of the principal sources of human upset and stress is the tendency to exaggerate negative emotions and judgements. It was not, I realised, terrible. It was inconvenient. It was annoying. It was frustrating. But it was not terrible. Inconvenient, annoying and frustrating rank relatively low on the distress scale. Terrible is about as high as you can get. When I acknowledged that, I still didn't like the fact that the office had been moved miles away from the very citizens who needed to use it. At least, though, I was not ramping up my anger and distress through my careless use of language and of thinking.

Perhaps the major principle we need to understand is that we have a tendency to exaggerate the way we speak to ourselves about our emotions. So instead of seeing something as inconvenient, we may see it as 'terrible', as I did.

How does this apply to the future? Once again, it's a matter of how we talk to ourselves. I might tell myself that it would be catastrophic if I didn't do well in my exam, whereas it would in fact be very unpleasant and disappointing but hardly catastrophic. It may mean I would have to go through the whole business of repeating the exam and of knuckling down again to studying. But catastrophic? No. If failing the exam meant I would lose my job, lose my house and be divorced, that would be catastrophic.

Similarly, I might tell myself that it will be 'awful' if I am late for such and such a meeting. But if it's inevitable that I am going to be late, then this language just doesn't help.

PARADES GET RAINED ON

Life has a habit of raining on your parade. Actually, life has a habit of raining on parades in general. But guess what? Parades get rained on all the time and while this can be unpleasant and challenging and difficult, that doesn't make it terrible.

Another example of distorted thinking and exaggeration that is particularly relevant here is the assumption that everything you do should be done well enough to impress all the people who are important to you. The problem here is that the people who are important to you are a diverse bunch; it is impossible to impress them all at the same time. Moreover, most of them would probably be satisfied with a performance that is 'good enough' rather than one that is as close to perfection as possible.

Mindfulness helps us to spot distorted thinking as it happens and to step away from it. We spend less time pursuing these patterns of thinking and more time in reality. Sometimes, it has to be said, that reality is painful. But we will find even painful realities much easier to cope with if we avoid exaggerating them.

TRY THESE

Here are two ways to step down from exaggerating negative emotions and judgements and put a stop to crazy thinking.

Observe calmly. Sit for a moment and look calmly at the things that you do not know about an upcoming event, such as a job interview. Notice the tendency to worry in an exaggerated way about how the interview will go – whether the interviewers will be hostile, for instance. Observe your breathing and your physical state as you contemplate this. Stay with your breathing long enough to allow it to settle down. Then ask yourself what, if anything, you need to do. If necessary, do something, even something small, to begin your preparation. If you can do nothing about the event, find something else to do that you like doing and that will hold your attention. When you spot an exaggeration floating across your mind, return your attention to whichever course of action you have decided upon.

Say 'running away'. What happens when you exaggerate the seriousness of a task or event is that you are allowing your mind to 'run away' with you. When you notice this happening, use a phrase like 'running away' to bring your attention back. Not only will such a phrase help to bring you back to reality but it also has a bonus: labelling your emotions and the activity in your mind tends to dampen down the amount of energy you put into them. So simply labelling that 'exaggerating' as 'running away' will withdraw energy from it.

It's a catastrophe!: I had a colleague once who at some stage during every working day would tell us that things were 'catastrophic' or 'disastrous'. Of course, the day never did turn out to be catastrophic or disastrous (unsatisfactory and frustrating yes, disastrous no). I was often struck, though, by the large and obvious amount of anxiety she generated in herself. If she had been able to use a mindful approach to reduce or cut out this exaggeration, her days could have been far more pleasant.

○ QUICK THOUGHT: Use mindfulness to counteract your human tendency to exaggerate your negative emotions.

REACTIVITY: REDUCE
AUTOMATIC STRESS

Adrian lives with a black cloud that hovers over his mind all the time. The cloud is made up of ever-present worry and anxiety. He is beginning to feel quite down from the realisation that the black cloud never really goes away. It's an experience I can recall from my own teenage years and it's an unpleasant one. Sometimes, Adrian finds, the worry gives him a headache.

Adrian's difficulty is that when he encounters a source of worry, alarm bells immediately begin to ring. In other words, he is overreactive. If he could learn to lower his level of reactivity then his quality of life would improve hugely, and the black cloud would gradually dissipate. First, though, he has to be convinced that this is worth doing. Sometimes, people who are overly reactive feel almost as though something bad will happen if they don't worry intensely. However, Adrian is now so sick of worrying that he is ready to make a change. One of the changes he needs to make is to cultivate mindfulness to help him to get out of the vicious circle in which he is caught.

People who, like Adrian, have a poor level of awareness are susceptible to being pulled and pushed by whatever is going on in their mind. It's as though they slam down the shutters on whatever they were doing as soon as that alarm bell rings. For such people, cultivating awareness will in itself reduce the amount of time they spend away from the present moment and lost in worry. They can develop that awareness through using the methods outlined in this book. Anything that develops mindful awareness will be of help to them.

ACCEPTING THE PRESENCE OF WORRIES

It isn't, of course, a matter of never having worries going through their minds. That, as I've outlined, is an impossibility. What really matters is to be able to accept the presence of worries without repeating and exaggerating them.

Take a person who worries a lot about what sort of assessment they will get from their manager at the end of the year. Until the suspense is over, the issue will return to their mind fairly often. The question is, what will they do with that worrying? What they could do is notice the presence of that worry while they get on with the job. They don't actually need to get rid of the thoughts them-selves. In fact, there is reason to believe that attempting to get rid of thoughts makes them persist. What they need is to accept that the thoughts are there but not engage with the story the thoughts are telling them. Gradually the thoughts will become less intense.

The experience of being less reactive is, of course, a key aspect and benefit of mindfulness. This has nothing to do with being callous or indifferent. Neither has it anything to do with taking the passion out of your life. It is a matter of bringing your awareness to your breathing or to your body instead of getting lost in the stories your worries tell.

From thoughts to activity: An effective way of tackling the habit of overreacting is to get yourself involved in activities that are of absorbing interest to you. The activity gives you a focus to help you avoid being pulled away by your worries and your thoughts. When the thoughts occur, simply practise returning to the activity on which you are attempting to concentrate. The more interesting the activity, the easier it will be to move away from the intrusive thoughts. This is not a matter of escapism; in effect, you are acknowledging the presence of the thoughts and then returning to your activity even though the thoughts may still linger. I would suggest that you choose a physical activity, such as gardening, painting, walking or sports. It is always easier to remain mindful of physical activities.

TRY THESE

Here are two simple mindfulness approaches to practise every day to help reduce a tendency to overreact to stress.

Practise 'small' mindfulness. As you go through your day, bring mindfulness to even the smallest tasks. You can start in the morning by doing an activity such as brushing your teeth with awareness. Indeed, you can start as soon as you get out of bed by switching to awareness of your feet against the floor. This helps you start the day without switching on the worry-machine in your head!

Accept your thoughts. Deliberately spend a few moments every now and then accepting thoughts and allowing them to pass. Suppose you have a family wedding coming up and the guest list includes relatives who really get on your nerves. Sit and allow your thoughts about the wedding to pass through your mind. As each one comes, notice it and then pass on to the next thought without comment. Do this for a few minutes, maintaining a background awareness of your breathing at the same time. Then turn your attention to whatever else you need to be doing right now. This teaches you that you can look at challenges without getting dragged away by worries in your head.

Break the spell: Adrian, and people like him, should probably focus on the first of these two approaches – basic mindfulness – or he could make use of the 'just worrying' technique (see 'Just Worrying: Don't amplify worry', on page 33) when worries arrive in his mind. In other words, he may need to use a couple of approaches to break the spell that worrying has exercised over him. But if he persists, he will see that black cloud give way to a blue sky.

○ QUICK THOUGHT: Develop present-moment awareness through mindfulness practice to calm an overreactive mind.

FORM THE INTENTION

Practice: Form the intention to be mindful first thing in the morning.

Commentary: It is said that intention is like the point of the needle: where the point goes, the thread follows. So make the intention first thing in the morning to approach your day with mindfulness. Mindfulness helps you to keep worries in perspective and especially to avoid losing yourself in them. When you know your intention (to write that report, buy the groceries on your shopping list and leave the supermarket to get home by 7 p.m., for instance), you stand a chance of doing what you meant to do without being lured away. The same applies to the intention to be mindful.

Tips: Quickly form the intention to be mindful before your feet touch the floor in the morning and whenever you are drinking a cup of tea or coffee during the day.

THE STRESS RESPONSE: CALMING YOUR ALARM SYSTEM

Martin had performed poorly in his last set of exams. This was unfortunate – his final results would determine whether he could get a place on the university course he wanted to do. He was spending time revising – many, many hours, in fact – but he had done particularly poorly in the pre-finals test, nevertheless.

A look at what was happening quickly reveals the problem. Martin was under extreme levels of stress and it didn't help that the teacher for his most difficult subject was herself suffering with high levels of stressful worrying, which she communicated to her class. Martin's parents were taking the view that if he did not get on to the course then his future would, essentially, be ruined. This was nonsense, of course, but that didn't stop them. They had also warned him that if he did not do well enough in the upcoming final exam, they would not be contributing further to his education. All of this, combined with Martin's self-imposed expectations, sent a clear 'alarm' message to his brain.

Stress, when intense enough, can shut down certain parts of the brain. When the brain notices that our stress levels have exceeded a certain point, it takes action on the basis that we may be in danger. To conserve our energies for fight or flight, it closes down activities such as digestion, the immune system and the learning system. When the stress levels fall, and the brain believes the danger is over, these systems are allowed to switch on again. In Adrian's case, the increasing stress that he was under had brought about exactly this effect and his learning capacity went out of the window. The shutting down of the immune system under extreme stress may also explain why very stressed people seem to get more infections.

THE STRESS CYCLE

It is useful to know about the stress cycle. This is a sort of vicious circle in which various components of stress can amplify each other. The cycle is made up of physical, emotional and cognitive responses. The word 'cognitive' refers to how we think. When we feel stress, we tense up emotionally; we experience a state of anxiety and our thinking gets locked into whatever we are stressed about. This thinking takes the form of rumination – worrying over and over about negative events or negative possibilities. The problem is that each of these can strengthen or stimulate the other. The part of that cycle that we tackle in mindfulness is rumination. I will say more about that later on in this chapter.

When we are stressed, we produce extra adrenalin and cortisol and that's a natural response. The problem is that if we are running adrenalin and cortisol all the time, the result is harmful rather than helpful. It's like leaving the tap running in your kitchen – useful while you need water, but the consequences if the water keeps flowing are not good. That steady drip of stress can increase the level of glucocorticoids in the stomach, which in turn can lead to gastric ulcers. The rumination that goes with high stress levels can contribute to depression.

Prolonged stress has a damaging effect on the cells that make up the body; you can read more about this in 'Getting into your genes: Why de-stressing matters' (see page 147).

Residual stress

I mentioned earlier that we increase production of cortisol when we are under stress. However, we also produce cortisol when we think about stressful events after they are over. Essentially, ruminating on past stressful events produces negative emotions, which switch on what's called the cortisol awakening response. So we experience stress both during events and when we relive them later in memory. People who practise mindfulness greatly reduce their rumination time – whenever they notice themselves ruminating, they step out of it. One of the benefits of this is that the cortisol response is awoken less often.

The part of your brain most affected by stress, anxiety

and worry is the amygdala. This is a small structure in the emotional or limbic region and it is concerned, among other things, with fight or flight. The amygdala carries a trace memory of anything that it has judged to be a source of danger to you in the past. Because of that, you can react instantly if you encounter that source of danger again. Worry, anxiety and stress all activate the amygdala and so, as I mentioned above, can thinking about past negative events. Once alerted, the amygdala triggers the stress response, including the production of cortisol and adrenalin. When you practise mindfulness consistently, your amygdala tends to calm down. Indeed, in people who practise mind-fulness consistently for a time, the amygdala even becomes a little smaller.

TRY THESE

Here are two more ways of working mindfully with these biological stress responses to calm your alarm system.

Focus on the out-breath now and then. The out-breath has a calming effect on our central nervous system, so if you're feeling tense or stressed in any of the ways mentioned above, put this to your advantage. Sit for a few minutes observing your out-breath and whenever your mind wanders off, bring it back. In this way, build episodes of calming your nervous system into your day.

Say 'not now'. When you catch yourself brooding on past negative events, you can return to awareness by silently saying 'not now' and returning your attention to your breathing. All of this will help to lower your stress response – that is, the production of cortisol. By the way, saying 'not now' doesn't oblige you to brood later – it's just a way to give your negative brooding the brush-off.

A good outcome: Martin's parents removed the threat not to fund his further education. They assured him that it would not be the end of the world if he had to repeat the exam the following year. Martin began to practise mindfulness to help with his general worrying. He could do nothing about his teacher's stress levels, but the measures he had taken enabled him to relax. This in turn allowed his brain to switch on its learning capacities to full force again, and his revision began to pay off. He passed his final exam with flying colours. When I next heard from him, he was halfway through his first year at university and loving it.

○ QUICK THOUGHT: Use mindfulness practice to lower the biological effects of stress and worry.

7/11 BREATHING

Practice: Breathe in to a count of seven and out to a count of eleven. So:

On the in-breath: 1, 2, 3, . . . 7

On the out-breath: 1, 2, 3, . . . 11

Commentary: Try this if you feel a little agitated or stressed and you want to calm yourself – though it's also quite a good mindfulness practice when you're not stressed. Making the out-breath longer tends to be especially calming. The counting gives your brain something to do instead of worrying.

Tips: If you find the '11' on the out-breath too long, reduce it to 9. It also helps to make the breath light and gentle as you do it.

INCREASE TOLERANCE: YOU CAN'T TAKE IT? YES YOU CAN!

I read an interview recently with a famous man whose dissatisfaction with everything was such that the journalist based his article on it. The man didn't like the coffee he was served; he didn't like the uneven pavement on the street as they walked to find better coffee; he didn't like having to wait in line for his lunch, so they skipped lunch; he didn't like the way people rushed about; and he declared that he didn't like television and he didn't like the movies. Although this man has had a good deal of what we perceive as success (a good career, plenty of money and so on), you can see that his life is a rather miserable one. You probably wouldn't want to share it. He is a man who desperately needs to learn the value of tolerance.

One of the great contributors to our mental health is the ability to tolerate the dissatisfactions of life. This is not about putting up with things that you should not put up with (and in my view, the more you practise mindfulness, the better you will get at separating what to tolerate from what to tackle). It's about being able to take a calm view of the many things in the day, in a relationship, or in ourselves that are not as we would like them to be.

ALL OR NOTHING THINKING

We are all guilty of what is called 'all or nothing thinking'. This is thinking that if one thing is wrong in a situation, then the whole situation is wrong. In the imperfect world in which we live, it's a way of thinking that can bring great unhappiness. But mindfulness can help by making us more at ease in this imperfect world.

Suppose you offer to organise a wedding for a friend. That's a task that is going to generate its own share of stress and anxiety, no matter how you go about it. But to preserve your sanity and that of others, you need to be able to do it without allowing the anxiety to take over. What does tolerating dissatisfaction mean in this context?

Suppose everything has been planned and you suddenly wonder if the dessert at the meal will be alright. Why would you wonder this? Well, when you yourself were getting married the hotel came up with a rather limp and unsatisfactory dessert. It upset your mother a great deal (she had taken on the task of organising your wedding) and led to a dramatic and embarrassing show-down between her and the banqueting manager right there in the room.

So suddenly this idea begins to niggle at you. What if they get the dessert wrong? Won't that be the only thing the guests will remember?

As you read this, you can see what an irrational sort of thinking that is – even if the dessert is below par, the guests will probably have forgotten about it quickly. And yet in the real situation it is all too easy to get caught up in anxiety and stress and to worry about such fairly unimportant things. Instead, you can simply accept that, despite your best efforts, not everything will go right. Accepting this, you can get on with doing the planning as best you can but without distressing yourself with worry over something that may never happen.

In another scenario, you can spend too much time and energy polishing a presentation because you fear that one thing will be wrong and everybody will notice that one thing. You get yourself so caught up in a ball of anxiety about this that a really important thought never occurs to you: the audience will be too busy absorbing the information in your presentation to notice minor imperfections. And if you are to get the presentation done on time, you may need to accept the dissatisfaction of knowing that minor imperfections occur.

TOLERANCE THROUGH MINDFULNESS

Through mindfulness, we learn to tolerate life's imperfections with good grace and to become less attached to

63

outcomes being exactly the way we want them to be. Essentially, this is about losing our attachment to the idea that something must be perfect – or else it will be completely unacceptable.

Let's look at some of the ways in which mindfulness helps us with this whole concept of increasing our level of tolerance.

Mindfulness lowers emotional reactivity

Our conviction that if something is wrong, everything is wrong is, to a large extent, an emotional reaction. As you will see in the chapter on biology (Anxious bodies: It isn't all in the mind, page 153), mindfulness reduces our emotional reactivity. It doesn't eliminate reactivity – which would, of course, be a bad thing – but what it does is to bring reactivity down to a level that is helpful to us. That is, to a level that gives us space to think and act effectively.

We become less anxious about perfection

If we know that we are going to be able to accept most of what our experience brings us and even most of the things about ourselves that we wish were different, everything changes. We don't have to wind ourselves up into a ball of anxiety, worrying whether things will be perfect – we simply accept that they won't be. In other words, we are not making perfection a condition of our enjoyment of life.

TRY THESE

Here are two mindfulness practices that can help to increase tolerance and prevent us falling into a pattern of 'all or nothing' thinking.

An hour of imperfections. For the next hour, notice imperfections and annoyances as you go about your business. This could be your slow computer, an irritating colleague, the noise of traffic – you'll find lots if you look, trust me! Practise tolerating these imperfections without criticising, either out loud or in your mind. Just sit with them, so to speak, moving your attention to your breath or posture if it helps. By doing this, you're building your level of tolerance of our imperfect world.

Notice and tolerate imperfections in your body. When doing an exercise such as the body scan (see Slow Body Scan, page 17), you are likely to encounter the imperfect aspects of your body. But don't criticise these imperfections – simply accept them as part of your experience and move on. This again helps to cultivate tolerance – it helps us to see that imperfection is part of the deal and that that's okay.

○ QUICK THOUGHT: Increasing your tolerance of imperfection and of the small things that annoy you can leave you free to get much more out of life.

HOW DOES THIS HELP ME?

Practice: Get into the habit of asking yourself now and then: 'How does it help me to have these thoughts?'

Commentary: Do you go over and over your own faults and mistakes and stress yourself out over them – a form of worrying about the past? Or after you have prepared as much as you can for an event, do you sit there worrying about it anyway? When you do something foolish, do you pace up and down, worrying about how you could have done such a thing? The likelihood is that this thinking is useless. Asking yourself 'How does this help me?' will often reveal instantly the uselessness of your thoughts. Instead, use your energy to do something fun or useful.

Tips: Make a deal with yourself that whenever you are sipping your tea, coffee or water, you will come out of your thoughts long enough to focus your attention on that sip. And now and then, during that space, ask 'How does this help me?', the 'this' being your worrying and thinking. That space, that sip, could become hugely important in reducing your level of worrying.

PART THREE: STOPPING THE WORRY SPIRAL

PROCESS NOT OUTCOME:
TAKING CARE OF 'HOW'

George was knowledgeable, conscientious and, by and large, his team liked him. He would have made a good team leader but for one fault: whenever the team had a big project in hand, he would get so caught up in worries about the outcome that it became impossible to get his attention. He was impatient with new ideas coming from other members of the team – they could see it in his pursed lips and averted eyes – and snapped at those who brought up difficulties late in the day.

This meant that George was not getting full value from his team. He missed out on their advice and their creativity. As a result, projects sometimes came to fruition with more flaws and less added value than they could have had. Moreover, George found himself leading a team whose members were glad to move to where their input was listened to and appreciated. And as time went on, he also began to notice the wear and tear on himself of the stress he was experiencing. His family suggested he go to counselling because of his irritability and because he was unable to sleep well any more. George took the opportunity to explore how he approached his work, and he quickly came to appreciate the value of focusing on process instead of outcome.

A BETTER OUTCOME

What lessons can you take from this? The first is to remember that preoccupation with the outcome removes your engagement with the present. Spend the day worrying about whether you will sleep well tonight and you will miss what the day has to offer. Worse, it removes your enjoyment in the daily details of your life. You could be the man driving through a beautiful landscape, worried about what time he will get to his destination and blind to the lovely scenery around him. That's why, if we want to improve the quality of our lives, we need to focus more on process and less on outcome – and mindfulness is process-oriented. For instance, we give attention to the process of breathing, of sitting, of walking and so on. This process-oriented awareness contributes at least as much to our quality of life as worrying about where we hope to be in five years' time.

Paradoxically, focusing on process produces better outcomes. This is because stress, produced by excessive worrying about outcomes, narrows our vision and reduces the range of possibilities that we can see. A focus on process usually lowers stress and thereby helps us to see possibilities we would otherwise have missed.

In mindfulness we give our awareness to process – to what we are doing now – and not to endless thoughts about outcome. Of course, we know the outcome we want. We know the sort of cake we want to bake but we need to pay attention to the baking!

TRY THESE

Here are some ways to use mindfulness practice to help you focus on process rather than outcome and to reduce worry and stress.

What's the next action? This idea is borrowed from productivity guru David Allen's Getting Things Done® system which focuses on the next, usually small, action you need to take towards your goal. For instance, if I want to cycle round the world, my next action might be to Google websites about cycling around the world. My action after that might be to list some points I've noticed when reading the websites. At some stage, my next action might be to ask my boss if I can have a year's leave of absence. The next action is almost always less stressful than worrying about the project as a whole. In this way, the outcome becomes the end point of a series of next actions. And each 'next' action, despite its name, is usually something I can do 'in the now'. For instance, if I want to ask my boss for that year's leave of absence, a next action might be to list some points I can make in the hope of persuading her.

Return, return, return. Mindfulness practice encourages us to keep returning our attention to what's going on now, rather than wandering off into the stories in our mind. This simple word 'return' is of huge benefit in helping us to focus on process. Whenever you wander off into thoughts about the outcome, return your attention to what you need to do right now to bring about that outcome. And what you need to be doing is the 'next action'.

The value of listening: In George's case, what needed to be done was to listen to his colleagues on the team. That was the rich source of valuable information and ideas that he was ignoring when he preoccupied himself with his worries about the outcome. After he had spoken to his counsellor, he began to respect process and to seek his team's views at every stage of a project. Soon, people wanted to join his team, not leave it.

◯ QUICK THOUGHT: Reduce worry about outcomes by switching your attention to the process of getting things done.

SLOW DOWN

Practice: Now and then today, slow down whatever you're doing and pay attention to your actions: drinking tea, entering a password, opening a door, say.

Commentary: This practice immediately takes you out of your worried head and into mindful awareness. Not only worry but also technology and the demands made by ourselves and others encourage us to rush ever faster. Sometimes it's a wonder we don't spin off into outer space! Slowing down to practise mindfulness is an act of self-assertion. It is saying, 'I am not on this Earth to keep up – my life means more than that.' It is pausing, every now and then, to bring myself into my own presence.

Tips: Continue this slow activity for longer. See also if you can bring about a slight slowing down of activities you engage in when other people are present – so slight that they don't notice, but you do. Your worries may be in the background but they will no longer dominate.

LOCKED IN: STAY OUT OF WORRY PRISON

When Margaret starts to worry, she *really* starts worrying. Her friends can actually see her worries progressing into a whole loop of worrying – it's as though she's climbed on a mental treadmill.

Margaret and her boyfriend are planning to travel around Europe by train, but when Margaret begins to talk about the arrangements, you can almost hear her clicking into 'worrying mode'. Her brow furrows and she gets a distant look in her eyes. Sometimes her friends make fun of her by waving their hands in front of her eyes, as if to take her out of a trance. Sometimes that even works. But as soon as Margaret is away from them, she gets completely locked on to her worries again. And in a very short time she moves from being locked *on to* them to being locked *in to* them.

LOCKED ON OR LOCKED IN: WHAT'S THE DIFFERENCE?

'Locking on' to an issue means focusing your attention on it. Getting 'locked in' means obsessing about it, and becoming consumed by it.

When we lock *on* to a problem, we need to maintain enough awareness of what we are doing to avoid getting locked *in*.

Not everybody gets locked in to worrying like this, of course. But if you're very used to worry it could become so habitual that you do indeed get locked in, and this is what happens to Margaret. Also, if you are a perfectionist you are at risk of getting locked in by worry – perfection is impossible to achieve, so the perfectionist always has something to worry about!

The big contribution mindfulness can make is to cultivate awareness of what is going on here. Once Margaret becomes aware that she is caught in a worry loop, she can begin to look for a better – that is, less stressful – way to relate to the holiday. She might check with her boyfriend and find that he isn't expecting precision timing. If he is, she might suggest that he organises the connections himself. What matters to us here are not the details of Margaret's story, but the fact that mindful awareness allows her to see a wider range of choices.

Here are two specific actions that can help get you – and Margaret – out of that 'locked in' trap.

Ask for fresh perspectives. When you get locked in to extreme, repetitive worry, you stop seeing fresh possibilities. You plod along the same old paths in your mind and the more stressed you get, the narrower your focus becomes. You may think you are exploring possibilities, but really you are in a trance in which you are relating only to what's going on in your own head. What you need to do is get a fresh perspective from inside somebody else's head.

You need to ask what other people think. When you do, you may discover that the issues you took so desperately seriously are not seen as serious by others; or that the perfectionistic demands you place on yourself are seen as silly by others. How bad would it be, one of Margaret's friends might ask, if arrangements went wrong and she and her boyfriend spent an extra night in a beautiful European city? She may find, to her surprise, that the demand that she gets it all 100 per cent right is coming from only one person – herself. Seeking fresh perspectives from people you know have your best interests at heart is an effective way of freeing yourself from the mental jail in which you've locked yourself.

Ask, 'Where is the plan?' Margaret needs to remind herself of the difference between planning and worrying. Planning means making the arrangements that she needs to make now, and seeking useful information from her boyfriend or someone else who can help, whereas worrying is simply a useless activity with which she fills her head with unhelpful 'what ifs'. When Margaret finds herself worrying, she can ask herself, 'Where is the plan?' The answer may be that the plan is already done (maybe she has already booked the trains but has kept on worrying anyway!) and she can give her attention to something else. The 'something else' could be the conversation she is meant to be having with her friends. If the answer is that she still has planning to do, then she needs to switch from worrying to working out the details of the plan.

Planning usually answers questions such as:

- What do I want?

- What do I need to do?

- How? Where and when? With whom?

When you plan, you end up with series of actions, times, places and, usually, people who can help.

○ QUICK THOUGHT: Use mindful awareness and mindfulness to help you avoid getting 'locked in' to worries.

TAKE A DETOUR

Practice: Park your worrying about a particular issue by taking a detour into a useful or fulfilling activity.

Commentary: Because we are problem-solving creatures, we can fall into the trap of thinking about problems beyond the point at which doing so is useful. We may be too tired to come up with an answer or perhaps the problem doesn't have a satisfactory solution, yet we go on thinking and worrying. Rest your mind by taking a detour into a more satisfying activity. Taking a detour might mean watching the box set you've been promising yourself for ages; working on a practical project to which you are already committed; meeting a friend for coffee; organising your study area, and so on. Whether or not you eventually arrive at a solution to your original problem, you will at least have got something useful or fulfilling done.

Tips: Instead of waiting until you are 'stuck' on a problem, figure out now a few activities that are useful or fulfilling and better than worrying. Do these activities when you want to take a detour.

THE ANXIETY, WORRY, STRESS TRIANGLE: WORKING WITH WORRY TO REDUCE STRESS

John and Richard are each doing an exam in the next couple of weeks. Both have a certain level of anxiety about the exam because they haven't prepared enough for it. John feels anxious and a little bit stressed and he deals with this by knuckling down to studying. But Richard feels very anxious and very stressed and he deals with this by worrying so much that he finds it impossible to study.

While John is experiencing a level of stress that is inevitable, Richard is amplifying his stress through worry and rumination.

So let's break this down a little.

Anxiety, as I have pointed out elsewhere in this book, is inevitable in life. But some of us amplify our anxiety by focusing on worrying, and that is what Richard has been doing. Instead of taking anxiety as a signal to deal with the problem, Richard takes it as a signal to worry. This is a common behaviour and in fact it's something that we seem to do almost as naturally as we feel anxiety. The problem is, worry amplifies stress.

AMPLIFIED STRESS

Suppose you're planning to ask your boss for six months' unpaid leave so that you can circumnavigate the United States on a bicycle. You're probably going to feel a certain level of anxiety and stress in the lead-up to this conversation. However, if you can keep your anxiety at that inevitable level, you can at least sit down and plan out your strategy to get a 'yes' from the boss.

If, however, you indulge instead in excessive worrying, ruminating on the possibilities of a confrontation with your boss, you will amplify your level of stress. As a result, you will reduce your chances of coming up with a sensible argument. Finding an effective argument requires a reasonably clear and cool head and that's very difficult to achieve in a state of extreme stress. Stress is the enemy of creativity.

So remember this key point about worry in challenging situations: some worry is inevitable, but too much amplifies stress in ways that work against you. Be especially vigilant if you are a person who has a habit of stressful thinking. And remember that if you practise mindfulness, your stress levels will be easier to control.

TRY THESE

Here are two ways in which you can apply mindfulness to help you work *with* stress to reduce worry.

Use the 'not now' or 'just worrying' technique. When worry is uselessly standing in the way of planning or implementation, form the habit of silently saying 'not now'. Then get on with what you need to do. In situations in which worry is generally bothering you – even if you are not working on anything specific – silently say 'just worrying'. That labelling in itself will withdraw energy from the worrying and enable you to step out of the cycle of excessive worrying.

Practise mindfulness of the body. When you're feeling very anxious and stressed, bringing your attention to your body really helps. You could become mindful of your feet, your hands, or even your entire body; you could become mindful of the sensation of walking, or standing. Moving your attention from your head and into your body is far easier than dealing with your anxious thoughts directly. Moreover, as we know, tension in your body contributes to stress as well as being an outcome of it. Awareness of your body usually calms it, and will thus reduce your level of stress.

○ QUICK THOUGHT: Worry amplifies stress. Mindfully redirect your attention from worrying to your posture or your breathing as a way to lower stress levels.

WHAT YOUR HANDS DO

Practice: For a while, switch your attention from what's happening in your mind to what your hands are doing and how they feel.

Commentary: Almost everything your hands do happens outside your awareness. Bringing your hands into awareness is a valuable mindfulness practice. It's also a good alternative to indulging worries and unhelpful thoughts in general. Our hands express so much – love, hate, artistry, craft, competence – that in many ways they are part of us in a truly central way. That's why hands are often used as symbols in religion or romance. That's why we hold hands, we put our face in our hands, we rub our hands gleefully. And that's why mindfulness of your hands is really mindfulness of your own self.

Tips: Notice your hands and also notice the sense of energy in your hands. You might experience this as a tingling in your palms. Try to bring that awareness to the next thing you do with your hands.

ACCEPTANCE: WHAT IT IS,
WHY IT MATTERS

David's doctor has told him that he is a 'functioning hypochondriac'. What he means is that David brings every twinge to the surgery, although it's been years since he has had anything that qualifies as an illness. But though he spends more time than the average person in the doctor's surgery, he functions well enough in life.

David's problem is that he is low on the capacity to accept what he does not like. That doesn't just apply to his health. Whenever he has to make a phone call to a utility provider, he gets himself into a fight with the call centre. He has never been able to accept that, like it or not, call centres are an unavoidable fact of life. That being the case, he would be better off trying to get himself to the end of the whole experience in good humour rather than bad.

If you told David that he would enjoy life more if he cultivated acceptance, he would tell you that he will cultivate acceptance when everything is acceptable. When he says this, he thinks he has said something funny, just like his doctor thinks that his 'functioning hypochondriac' joke is funny. And just like his doctor, David chuckles to himself at his joke and fails to notice that nobody is laughing.

David's absolute refusal to cultivate acceptance means mindfulness would be a real challenge for him. Mindfulness is about returning your attention again and again to your breath, your physical senses, whatever reality is bringing you in the moment. But that's not all it is. Mindfulness also requires cultivating acceptance of whatever it is you are returning your attention to. What, after all, is the point of practising returning your attention again and again only to be immersed in stressful and painful thoughts? And David's thoughts and reactions are stressful. You only have to look at him to realise that. He has the permanent look of a man who finds his world unsatisfactory.

The problem for someone like David is that acceptance is one of the most difficult concepts in mindfulness practice. It doesn't mean agreement and it doesn't mean dismissing the impact of hurtful events that happen to us. What does it mean? The following are some possibilities, but first a true event . . .

Many years ago, somebody 'borrowed' a pocket watch from me. They didn't tell me they were 'borrowing' it and they didn't give it back. Another person was able to confirm my suspicions as to who the guilty party was but the guilty party had moved on and so there was no possibility of getting the watch back. As its value was largely sentimental, the thought of going to the police never occurred to me. I really liked the watch and I still miss it on the rare occasions on which I think about it.

ACCEPTANCE AND THE WATCH

What does acceptance have to do with the watch? Well, the loss of the watch doesn't interfere with my life because I know that the only thing I can do with that loss is accept it. So here are some thoughts on acceptance and the watch.

Acceptance is awareness without interference

We interfere with our awareness largely through self-talk and, to a lesser extent, talking to other people. When I remember the watch, I feel a dart of loss – but I don't fire another dart by talking to myself or anyone else about the watch. The feeling of loss passes as quickly as it arrives.

Acceptance means not deliberately rerunning an experience in the mind

I choose not to repeat to myself the story of the watch, the loss, and the judgements about it all (what a rotten thing to do, etc.). Instead, I acknowledge and feel the loss and then move forward. Which brings me to . . .

Acceptance is a way of relating to our experience that enables us to move forward with today and tomorrow

I could relate to the loss of the watch by dwelling on the story and the feelings surrounding the story. Instead, I allow myself to feel the feeling and then move on to the next thing I need to do.

If David were to read this, he would tell me I'm a fool and that I should have gone to the police about the watch. He might even say that because of my attitude, I deserved to lose the watch. So David and I will never agree on the value of acceptance.

Yet acceptance is one of the most rewarding life skills we can cultivate. Perhaps that's because it's one of the earliest lessons we get in life. As a child, you have to learn to accept that you cannot have dessert instead of dinner; that you cannot have all the toys; that you cannot go around thumping children you don't like; and that you have to go to bed, even though you think this is the most unjust thing in the world.

So acceptance is, actually, hard-wired into us through our earliest childhood experiences. But because acceptance is usually about putting up with what we don't like, we probably never deliberately cultivate it as a valued skill – not until we begin to practise an approach like mindfulness or until maturity brings us (if we're lucky) a degree of wisdom.

I'm not saying, of course, that all worry should be replaced by acceptance. If I am worrying about getting my tax returns done on time, and if we are approaching the eleventh hour, then I am right to worry. In this case, worrying will make me get a move on, get the figures out, and get the returns filled in. But suppose I am worrying about whether one of my colleagues will make dismissive remarks about a proposal I have put forward. Suppose that is what my colleague does every single time she receives a proposal from anyone. Then the worry is useless. I need to accept that this is her way, and move my attention away from the worry and on to something useful.

Cultivate acceptance every day: Acceptance can greatly reduce our level of worry. One way to cultivate acceptance is to quieten the mind and learn to observe experiences for a little while without self-talk. Practise on experiences like the bus being late or the weather being unpleasant. If you can accept the smaller things, this will stand you in good stead when bigger challenges come along.

TRY THESE

Here are two ways to bring an attitude of acceptance into your day by answering a simple question.

Ask, 'what should I worry about and what should I accept?' This is as simple as making a list, and distinguishing between those issues you need to accept (the late arrival of a present you ordered to give to a friend this weekend and now it's too late, so there's nothing to be done about it) and those that might be worth a little thinking about (getting the roof fixed before the winter rains arrive if you've been putting it off all summer). Eventually, you won't have to sit down and make a list any more: you just get better at making that valuable distinction on the go.

Ask, 'what do I need to accept about today?' In any given day, you will face a number of tasks or situations that you don't particularly like. Perhaps you have to drive through heavy traffic to get to a meeting; perhaps you know that this meeting, which you have little option but to attend, will be a complete waste of time. Worrying about it by running images of the traffic and of the meeting through your mind is pointless. Acceptance doesn't mean that you will like the drive or the boring meeting; it just means that you won't waste time and energy complaining and fantasising about these events. Just accept it and get on with it. And if you're going to fantasise, at least find something interesting to fantasise about!

A **secret worth knowing:** David could improve his experience of life if he were prepared to give acceptance a try. He would realise that he doesn't have to spend his life on a battlefield or in a state of anxiety about his health. In fact, if he would realise the value of acceptance he could probably remove 90 per cent of the stress that he now experiences. Acceptance is a secret worth being in on.

○ QUICK THOUGHT: Mindfulness doesn't just mean being 'in the now' but being in the now with acceptance, which is one of the greatest gifts of mindfulness.

ONE DAY OF ACCEPTANCE

Practice: For a day, experiment with accepting whatever comes your way.

Commentary: Remember that this doesn't mean rolling over and letting people walk on you. It means bringing a quiet mind to events instead of losing yourself in critical self-talk about them. If you find yourself ranting away in your mind, return your attention to your breath. Notice that many of the happenings you complain about don't really matter and are not worth getting upset over. Notice also how staying out of that ranting mind makes you far more effective in dealing with issues that really do matter.

Tips: One fascinating acceptance trick is to pretend to yourself, no matter what happens, that you chose it. This may seem daft but you will be surprised at how much of your experience you do actually choose. Who was it who put off driving to the shops until the evening rush hour? Why, it was you! Remember, this is a trick — I don't really want you going around thinking you've made it rain, but it's a very illuminating trick that can deepen your capacity for acceptance.

EMOTIONS: ACCEPT EVERY FEELING

In the previous chapter, I talked about the importance of being able to accept situations. Indeed, acceptance is a major theme of this book. That's because acceptance is a major aspect of mindfulness.

But sometimes what we find hard to accept is our own feelings – and that inability to accept feelings becomes a source of worry and anxiety in itself. That's why, in this chapter, I want to look at acceptance of feelings.

John has left it right to the last minute to finish a project – again. As he sits at his desk late at night, he can look down on the street and see other people making their way home after an evening out. Why has he allowed this to happen again? The project wasn't all that complicated and his fears of failing to complete it have, as usual, turned out to be groundless.

What has happened to John is that he has not learned to tolerate his physical and emotional feelings. These are the feelings that he has been experiencing since the project landed on his plate. Because he could not tolerate these feelings, he filled the space with worry. He made matters worse by distracting himself with less important tasks until the deadline loomed.

WHAT IS A 'PHYSICAL AND EMOTIONAL' FEELING?

What do I mean by physical and emotional feelings? I mean the physical feeling you experience when you think of something that has an emotional 'kick' to it. For instance, when you think about getting to Friday afternoon, finishing work and having a weekend off, you may have a feeling of lightness. On Sunday night, as Monday morning looms, that may be replaced by a physical sense of heaviness.

Very often, when we think of projects or issues or tasks that make us a little nervous, our nervousness shows itself in a physical dart of tension. Often you find that dart of tension located in your stomach.

When we cannot tolerate our own physical or emotional feeling – in this case, that dart of tension – then we have to get rid of it somehow. And we often get rid of the feeling temporarily by distracting ourselves with something less important, as John has been doing. For many of us, though, the distraction involves worrying. 'Can't you see I'm worrying about the issue?' we seem to say. 'What more do you want?'

However, if you can allow the dart of tension to occur, and can proceed without having to get rid of it, you can address the issue. As you continue to work, the tension will die down and perhaps even fade away altogether.

Becoming mindful of physical and emotional feelings, without seeking to escape them, is a major step towards allowing ourselves to take action on our various projects without building up a wall of extra worry about them.

It's not all about projects. Suppose I cannot tolerate the feeling of boredom? In that case, I mooch around miserably or restlessly looking for something to take the feeling away. But if I can accept boredom, perhaps I can allow myself to rest, to deliberately relax, and allow the feeling to pass in its own time. I may not be having fun, but neither will I be going around in circles, or eating or drinking too much, to escape that bored feeling.

I've mentioned before that acceptance of feelings is a key aspect of mindfulness practice. In mindfulness, you are not asked to do anything complicated with thoughts and feelings, such as get rid of them. You just notice them, and accept them.

TRY THESE

Here are two ways in which you can put into practice accepting every feeling, whether physical, emotional, or a combination of the two.

Practise experiencing emotions in your body. Sit and tune in to any tensions you notice. What emotions do you think they might be attached to? Having noted that, just observe the tensions as they change in intensity. Do so without in any way trying to get rid of them. Instead, observe them with curiosity. Do this for a couple of minutes at a time. In this way, you will gradually train yourself to accept your emotions by accepting the physical feelings that go with them.

Bring physical awareness into your work. As you are working on a project, allow yourself to be aware of the physical sensations that you feel as you are doing that work. Let them be there in the background, again without any need on your part to get rid of them. They will fade gradually as you continue with the work.

○ QUICK THOUGHT: Learning to accept and tolerate feelings of anxiety can free you to get on with what you need to get on with.

DELIBERATE BOREDOM

Practice: Sit for three minutes with the intention of doing nothing whatsoever, including thinking.

Commentary: This is an excellent direct training in taking your attention away from thinking and putting it on to something else, in this case doing nothing. And as you'll find, some of the thinking we do is no better than doing nothing; and sometimes doing nothing is better than the thinking we do. This is also a simple way to assert yourself in a world that demands your attention every second of the day from the moment you open your eyes to the moment you fall asleep.

Tips: Keep bringing your attention to the physical sensation of sitting, doing nothing. Every time your mind tries desperately to escape into thinking, pull it back gently to the sensation. When you feel an urge to get up and walk away, note the urge and return to the sensation.

PART FOUR: DEALING WITH THE NEGATIVE

HOLDING ON: LIGHTEN ATTACHMENTS TO LIGHTEN WORRY

Do you have a favourite restaurant? Let's suppose you have, and that you have a favourite table in that restaurant. The table is by a window that overlooks a pretty harbour. When you think about that table, and about the view of the harbour, you look forward to getting back there to have a really peaceful lunch. You could say that you're attached to sitting at that table and enjoying that view. Nothing wrong with that.

Now, suppose you ring the restaurant one day to make a booking and you discover that somebody else has reserved 'your' table. You explain how much you like the view, but the restaurant explains that the table has been booked by a regular customer with an important client. The customer booked the table so that the client would enjoy the view and be suitably impressed.

You ask to speak to the owner. The owner explains that the restaurant will not change the booking. You declare that you will never set foot in their restaurant again.

The owner says she's sorry you see it like that and that you can have any other table in the house, but the conversation ends without agreement.

You go back in future, nevertheless, because you really like that view, but you never feel quite as happy there again. In fact, whenever you think of booking the table you feel a dart of anxiety: will 'they' disappoint you again?

'QUALITY WORLD'

Your problem is attachment. You have become so strongly attached to sitting at that table that you cling to the idea. If you like, you're clinging to the table. If this were a cartoon, we would see you holding on to the table leg while the owner and the waiter tried to haul you away by your ankles.

Attachments are made up of the people, experiences and objects we want, that we make efforts to get, and that we miss if we don't have them. Dr William Glasser, who developed Reality Therapy, described all of those attachments as making up your 'quality world'.

Your quality world doesn't only include noble preferences, like world peace or being kind to puppies. It could include pleasures such as ice cream, steak or coffee; and not only ice cream, but a certain brand; not only steak, but a fillet steak medium rare; not only coffee, but that coffee, made by that barista, in *that* café beside your workplace. And maybe not any barista, but that *particular* barista!

Whatever gets into your quality world gets there for all sorts of reasons outside the scope of this book. But, probably, most of your preferences were formed so quickly that you didn't even notice what was happening at the time. For instance, that view from the harbour that you so enjoyed instantly became part of your quality world. Now, it's okay to like the view; it's the clinging that does the harm. That's what creates worry, stress and anxiety.

The trouble with clinging

To cling to an attachment can harm your relationship with others around you and destroy your peace of mind. Suppose you have an attachment to the wish that when your daughter goes to college in another city she should be safe and happy. Fair enough and understandable enough. But suppose clinging to this attachment means ringing your daughter incessantly. Suppose you get on a train when she becomes so fed up she stops answering the phone. Suppose you inspect her accommodation and try to vet her new friends. Suppose you demand that she gets one of those apps for her phone that will enable you to know where she is at all times, just in case.

But isn't your daughter's safety a worthwhile attachment? Yes – in fact, it will always be one of your strongest attachments. But if you cling too closely to that attachment, in the ways outlined above for instance, you will live in a welter of worry and stress. And your actions could quickly lead your daughter to avoiding contact with you.

In other words, clinging can lead to the loss of the very thing you are attached to. Clinging also takes the good out of experiences you could enjoy if your grip were lighter. Perhaps you could enjoy the restaurant now and then without the view; perhaps you could enjoy being part, at a distance, of your daughter's experiences without over-whelming her. That's why attachment and clinging are important concepts in the mindfulness approach. When you cling, you don't live in the present. You live in a fictional future in which you either do or do not get what you so desperately want. Because you are obsessed with a fictional future, you turn your back on your own life today.

So we need to learn to lighten our hold on attachments. How attached are you to what's in your handbag, your briefcase, your pocket, your house, your office, whether because of their actual use or their emotional meaning? The more attachments you have, the more anxious you have to be about safeguarding these attachments. Protecting is good, but try to protect without clinging.

TRY THESE

Here are two ways to help you lighten your hold on attachments, personal or material, in order to lighten worry.

Do an attachment check. When you feel anxious about something in your day, quickly check if you might be more attached to the outcome than is necessary. Do you get into a ball of tension about the state of your teenager's bedroom? Could you have become over-attached to the idea of your teenager having an untypically neat and clean room? Can you let go of that a little?

Accept that your control is limited. Fundamental to the practice of mindfulness is the understanding that much of what goes on in our world is outside our own control. If we can accept this fact, then we can worry less about perfection and predictability. I might want you to be impressed when you read my report; however, I need to accept that after I have given it my best shot, your attitude will still be somewhat unpredictable. You may have had a row with your partner, which put you into a bad mood before you read it, for example!

○ QUICK THOUGHT: Learn to like without clinging.

LISTEN TO THE CHATTER

Practice: Listen to the chatter in your mind without getting involved.

Commentary: What's going on in your mind? Reruns of old memories? Criticisms and judgements? Images? Movies? Worries about the future? If you watch for a minute or so every now and then, you will be surprised at the extent to which the mind recirculates the same material. To be able to observe all this going on without getting caught up in it can help you to step out of old preoccupations and cultivate a sense of detachment for when you need it most.

Tips: Choose a five-year period in your life and observe what your mind brings you by way of memories and feelings about that period. Consider how much more happened in that time than the little you recall now. Can you remember what you were worried about then? Can you remember more than a few worries? Notice how worries and memories fade into the past. Are you sure you need to take all today's worries quite so seriously?

EXTREME ANXIETY: PANIC ATTACKS AND OTHER CONDITIONS

While the focus of this book is worry, I want also to address the dilemma of people who suffer extreme levels of stress and anxiety. Examples might include what is known as generalised anxiety disorder, social anxiety, panic attacks, phobias and obsessive-compulsive disorder.

The word 'disorder' is the medical terminology, but really these are aspects of the human experience at the more troublesome end of the scale. The people who experience these difficulties are not, themselves, 'disordered'.

Mindfulness cannot take away these conditions, but mindfulness practice can most certainly help by changing how you relate to your anxiety. And while mindfulness is not the complete answer, it can make a valuable contribution to improving your sense of well-being. The following explores briefly how mindfulness can help.

GENERALISED ANXIETY DISORDER (GAD)

People who experience generalised anxiety disorder have higher than average levels of anxiety most of the time. Their anxiety doesn't have to have a logical source. It can hit without any apparent cause. And in any case, if one issue about which the person is anxious is resolved, the anxiety just moves on to another. Many of us might feel anxiety if, say, we have a deadline coming up that we're in danger of missing, but the person with GAD may have that same level of anxiety even without that deadline. It's as though their anxiety goes around seeking a target at all times.

People who suffer with GAD will find two key aspects of mindfulness helpful. The first is learning how to come out of rumination and brooding and the second is practising mindful acceptance.

Ruminating and brooding on matters you might feel anxious about make anxiety worse. Instead, when you notice you are brooding, return to mindful awareness. Most people return to awareness of breathing, but I would suggest as an alternative that you bring your awareness to your feet (especially if awareness of your breathing makes you feel nervous). Your feet are as far away from your head as you can get!

Combine awareness with acceptance of thoughts and feelings. Simply accept that this anxiety is here. Don't make matters worse by getting anxious about being anxious. Whenever you feel anxiety, your mind will seek an explanation for it. For instance, you might tell yourself that having to go to work makes you nervous as soon as you wake up in the morning. It is entirely possible, though, that this is the wrong explanation, and that your anxiety may be self-triggering and nothing to do with going to work. Better to say 'oh, there's anxiety' and to bring your attention back to your actions than to get caught up in ruminating on it.

I want to make a distinction here between ordinary and generalised anxiety. As we know, 'ordinary' anxiety can be useful; but generalised anxiety doesn't have helpful aspects because it is self-triggering. It is in this case that moving from speculating on the cause of the anxiety to an awareness of your body can help.

SOCIAL ANXIETY

People with extreme social anxiety experience more than mere shyness or embarrassment in social situations. They will go to great lengths to avoid finding themselves in these uncomfortable and upsetting situations. At the same time, because they are human and live in an interconnected world, they need social interaction.

So the person with social anxiety might dutifully attend every meeting they have to attend at work but avoid social interaction afterwards. Indeed, other workers might see them as stand-offish, never realising that they are, in fact, extremely shy.

How can mindfulness help? Mindfulness encourages people with social anxiety to go into social situations *accompanied* by their anxiety. To say you will go to parties or meetings when your anxiety disappears is to give yourself a life sentence. Unless you enter these situations, your anxiety will never disappear. Exposure to what you are anxious about is a key treatment for anxiety (for more on this, see the chapter 'Exposure: Experience fears to face them down', page 189). Moreover, you may find that you will always be more anxious than average in social situations – but not at the extremely painful level involved in social anxiety. That makes it all the more important to be able to tolerate the anxiety and have a social life nonetheless. How are you supposed to do all this? One way is to remain aware of your breathing and of symptoms such as your heart pumping as you go into social situations. Gradually, you will be able to get more and more involved in these situations as your tolerance level grows and your anxiety is less easily triggered.

It's really important also to remember that you don't have to be the life and soul of the party. Sometimes, people with social anxiety measure themselves against the most extroverted person in the room – better to measure yourself against the average person or even the average quiet person. I would also encourage you to be more mindful of the other people in the room than of yourself. Socially anxious people tend to give excessive and painful attention to themselves and to how they are coming across. Switch your attention to the other people, to what they're talking about, what they think of things (ask questions), or what they do, and bear in mind that you don't have to say terribly clever things in conversation. Listen mindfully and you will find that, 99 per cent of the time, people are saying very ordinary things – I suggest you do the same.

PANIC ATTACKS

Panic attacks are deeply unpleasant experiences, which occur in a variety of situations. Symptoms are many and they can vary from person to person. They can include breathlessness, sweating, nausea, feeling faint, fast heartbeat, weakness in the legs and a sense of dread. Often when people find a panic attack beginning, they – quite naturally – try to escape from the situation in which it is occurring, and if it occurs in situations that are hard to get out of, then they try to avoid those situations in the future. This might include avoiding travelling on a train or bus or walking into shopping centres.

The problem here is that a panic attack doesn't necessarily have a logical trigger. Panic attacks can be quite irrational. The situation in which the panic attack occurs may not be the cause of the panic attack itself. Some evidence suggests, for instance, that a panic attack can begin to build an hour or more before you notice the symptoms. Panic attacks may be related to changes in the balance of oxygen and carbon dioxide in the blood, caused by very fast breathing; however, they remain a mystery, even though, in our highly stressed era, they are more common than you might think.

So having a panic attack doesn't mean something unusual is wrong with you. It doesn't mean that you are 'going mad', as people sometimes fear. And it won't harm you physically, although it produces unpleasant physical symptoms. The main harm that panic attacks do is to limit your choices: you avoid going to certain places or having certain experiences for fear of also going into a panic.

How can mindfulness help with panic attacks? Essentially by enabling us to tolerate them as they are happening. When we notice a panic attack kicking in, it is natural to respond with the thought that this is terrible and I must escape from it. Such thinking, however, can have the effect of making the panic attack worse. Instead, learn to observe the panic attack as it rises and falls. Notice changes in the intensity of the symptoms as this goes on. Imagine that you are actually curious about the panic attack and what it's like. The panic attack itself will probably rise and fall in twenty minutes at most. It still won't be a pleasant experience, but you will learn not to fear it so much. This change in attitude will free you up to do many things that you had previously avoided. You will also find, if you follow this advice, that panic attacks will come less often and be less intense. This is especially so since mindfulness, if practised consistently, will lower your overall levels of stress.

PHOBIAS

Phobias can have causes that we don't remember – these causes may be lost in childhood, for instance. As with many other anxiety problems, exposure to what you are afraid of is a key to recovery. Suppose, for instance, that you have a phobia about cats. A gradual exposure might begin with looking at pictures of cats. In doing so, notice the sensations of nervousness and continue until the sensations die down. Next, you might allow yourself to look at the real cat from some distance away and gradually approach it. Continue to work in this way until you are able to touch the cat without fear.

How can mindfulness help with this? Very often, what we are afraid of is our own sensations of fear. In mindfulness, you learn to observe these sensations calmly. As I mentioned earlier, this is, in itself, a form of exposure to what you are afraid of. Remember, though, that when dealing with a phobia you mustn't try to do everything at once. If you do, you will be flooded by fears that will simply drive you away. The exposure must be very, very gradual, and in that way you take two important steps: you allow yourself to feel a level of fear that you are able to tolerate, and you give that fear the opportunity to die down.

OBSESSIVE-COMPULSIVE DISORDER (OCD)

Anybody who suffers from OCD will know that anxiety, along with obsessive thoughts, is at the very heart of it.

Sometimes, the OCD is a way of managing or avoiding extreme anxiety or just relieving it. Cleaning the house when you are stressed out is an example of this at a fairly harmless level, but spending so much time cleaning the house that you have little time for anything else is obsessive. So is checking twenty times that you switched off the fire before you went to bed. As in the case of phobias, use mindfulness to experience your anxiety without desperately trying to get rid of it. You may need other help as well, for instance through Cognitive Behaviour Therapy, which is outside the scope of this book. The key point, though, is that the more you can tolerate anxiety, the less you will need to get away from it by indulging in certain behaviours.

Seeking help: If you suffer from any of the extreme forms of anxiety, it's clear that mindfulness can help. But that doesn't mean mindfulness is the only answer or that mindfulness on its own is sufficient. I would urge you to seek help, whether from a counsellor or a doctor or both, in addition to using mindfulness as a tool.

TRY THESE

Here are two mindfulness practices that may be particularly helpful for those who suffer with any of these extreme forms of anxiety.

Walk mindfully. Mindful walking means walking at a pace that allows you to be aware of your actual walking. You don't have to walk unnaturally slowly. The key is to bring your awareness back to your walking again and again. Mindful walking is especially good if you feel agitated.

Labelling. The mindfulness technique of labelling your experiences has a great deal to offer to people suffering extreme anxiety. When you find yourself thinking anxious thoughts, label them silently in your mind with the word 'thinking' or 'anxious' or even 'fearful' and then go on with what you're doing. When you do this, you withdraw energy from that anxiety.

○ QUICK THOUGHT: Use mindfulness to help you regain control of your life if you experience extreme forms of anxiety.

TAKE A WALK

Practice: Go for a mindful walk and continually move your attention from your worries to the walking experience.

Commentary: Walking will generally lift your mood if you allow it. That means experiencing the walk rather than the world in your head. You can walk around a park, around the block, sometimes around your home or your workplace. This is an old mindfulness practice, valued because paying attention to the walking can really get you into the moment.

Tips: Notice your feet against the floor or ground, notice the movement of your body through the space in which you are walking. If your hands are moving by your sides, notice the sensation of air against them. As thoughts occur, acknowledge their presence and bring your attention back to walking.

SITUATION, THOUGHTS, FEELINGS: WHERE TO INTERVENE

Michelle is being bullied by a colleague at work. The colleague had never liked Michelle but her dislike went out of control when Michelle was promoted over her. Now the colleague refuses to accept instructions from Michelle. She has been known to laugh in her face in front of others when Michelle gives an instruction. She encourages her colleagues to ignore Michelle's wishes. Michelle's boss is unwilling to do anything about this. The bully worked for the founder of the company, now retired, and, in Michelle's opinion, her boss is afraid to tackle her. Michelle wants to use mindfulness to help her cope with the extreme distress that this situation is putting her under.

The problem here is that what has destroyed Michelle's peace of mind isn't only her thinking – it's also the situation she is in, which she seems powerless to change. Mindfulness will help but, really, for as long as she is in the situation, she is going to find it difficult.

Michelle's worry and stress can be seen as having three

components. These are the situation, her thoughts and her feelings.

Clearly, if we are in a situation that's distressing, we will feel distressed. The way we think about the situation can affect the level of stress we experience, but it doesn't prevent the existence of stress in itself. Some thoughts are useful, of course – for instance, thoughts that help Michelle to work out how to deal with the situation. But they become unhelpful if she continuously reruns scenes from her work-place in her mind, morning, noon and night.

Essentially, Michelle needs to relate to her thinking in a way that helps her. She needs to be able to accept her feelings, because her feelings are not really under her direct control. And she needs to take effective action about the situation. Sometimes, that means leaving the situation.

HOW CAN MINDFULNESS HELP?

Thoughts: Mindfulness can help Michelle by encouraging her, when she reruns scenes of bullying in her head, to switch her attention to her immediate reality. If she's in her kitchen cooking, that's her immediate reality. Her breathing is also her immediate reality. Through mindful-ness practice, Michelle can find a way of stepping out of being consumed by her thinking about what's happening in the office. By moving from obsessive thinking to mind-fulness, she can use her time outside work to recover and nourish herself.

Feelings: Michelle also needs to learn to accept her feelings without spinning off into distressing memories and fantasies about what could happen. To do this, she needs to bring her attention to the physical component of her feelings – a tightness in her chest, perhaps – rather than the thoughts that are triggered by her feelings. If she does this, she will see how feelings change intensity and how gradually, if she watches them and breathes calmly, they will ease.

Situation: As regards the situation itself, I would suggest that Michelle stays in touch with her breath while she is at work and while the bullying is going on. This will give her some control over her own reactions – and that may be all that is under her control in this situation. It might also give her enough emotional distance to assess whether what she needs to do is leave the situation. People who are being bullied in an organisation in which those in charge refuse to take action may very well need to leave if there is no prospect of ending the bullying. Is this unfair? Yes, but sometimes they need to put their own emotional and physical health first. If Michelle leaves, mindfulness can help her accept her thoughts and feelings about the situation, and any future memories of the bullying, so that she does not continue to be consumed by it.

A key point I want to make here is that mindfulness should not be used to keep yourself in a situation that you need to get out of. Instead, use mindfulness as a guiding hand to deal with the situation in the way that is best for you.

TRY THESE

Here are the two key mindfulness practices to help you in a difficult situation. If you use these, you may find that the situation is tolerable after all or you may intuitively arrive at a solution. On the other hand, you may come to the realisation that you need to leave the situation.

Practise returning to your immediate reality. If a situation and the thoughts surrounding it are particularly difficult and distressing, I suggest choosing a physical activity on which to focus your attention. This could be the sensation of walking or the feeling of your feet against the floor. Bringing your attention to your feet can be very helpful when your emotions are running very strongly. It can be very grounding.

Practise observing your feelings without being hijacked by them. A way to do this is to move your attention to the physical aspect of your feelings and observe these as if curious about them, while breathing calmly. If you do this, feelings of distress will usually subside and you will be less likely to be carried away by negative thinking.

> **Taking care:** Michelle does not have to be a prisoner of the situation in which she finds herself. Mindfulness can help her to see this as well as helping her to take the best care she can of her own mental and emotional health.

○ QUICK THOUGHT: **Mindfulness will not make an intoler-able situation tolerable, but it can help you to take the best possible care of yourself for as long as you have to stay in the situation, and afterwards.**

PART FIVE: GETTING IT RIGHT OR GETTING STUCK?

ALWAYS IN BETA: LIFTING THE CURSE OF PERFECTIONISM

Jane doesn't gets things finished. She didn't finish her degree; when she was given an important project to do at work, it had to be completed by a colleague; and she left the wallpapering of her hall half-done.

George always finishes whatever he takes on. He has a reputation for taking longer over projects than anybody else at work because he is so keen to get them absolutely right. He stays at the office late into the evening and often comes in at weekends. Still, the more important projects seem to go to other people. They get the work done more quickly, although with flaws that really annoy George. His home is decorated to perfection and it angers him excessively when the children leave finger-marks on the wallpaper or scratches on the furniture. He completed both his degree and his Masters with flying colours.

A SHARED AFFLICTION

What do Jane and George have in common? They both suffer from the same affliction: perfectionism. Both suffer worry, stress and anxiety because of it.

If the curse of perfectionism afflicts you, then you expect yourself to get everything more 'right' than it ever needed to be. The adequate report you could have sent yesterday is delayed while you tweak the colour on the charts; it's Christmas Eve and you're still searching for the perfect present; you get three firsts and one 2.1 in your essay results for a semester and you fret about that 2.1.

Or maybe you're a finisher: you get close to 'completely right' but at the cost of long hours, headaches, and possibly frustrating other people. All that to achieve a level of perfection nobody has actually demanded.

But what's wrong with the desire to do well? Nothing. To aspire to do well is good and results in very good work. To aspire to do perfectly, though, is to stress yourself out over an impossible demand. Worse, it can very easily result in nothing getting done, as nothing will ever reach your level of perfection.

And not only is the work not getting finished but, if you are mindful, you can quickly spot the physical effects of perfectionism: that hunched-over tightness in your neck and back muscles, a tightness that can extend to your chest and stomach muscles; and a sort of tunnel vision, with narrowed eyes, focused more on a detail that is wrong than on all that is right. It's a wonder you can perform at all in these circumstances.

But perfectionism has, I think, a more pernicious aspect: that is its ability to fool people who do good work into thinking they do bad work. Have you met people who do very good work indeed but whose perfectionist nature prevents them from acknowledging this? They worry about the 'bad' work they do while the rest of the world admires their achievements. These people include talented musicians who think they are not very good at music; gifted teachers who feel they let their students down; wonderful parents who believe they are failing their children; and good and effective therapists who feel they are failing their clients. All have in common that the work they do is very good quality – but it's never good enough in their eyes.

> **The failure in the mirror:** To see somebody going through life producing good work but thinking that they are not good enough saddens me. That's another aspect of the curse of perfectionism – it robs people of the satisfaction they could otherwise derive from what they do well. When they look in the mirror, they see a failure.

COMPASSION: FOR OTHERS AND SELF

Compassion, a key aspect of mindfulness, combats this sort of judgement. What is compassion? Compassion essentially involves a fellow feeling, an empathy, for others. This is usually accompanied by a desire that the other person should not suffer even though, sometimes, the suffering cannot be avoided. Most parents feel compassion for their child's anxiety on the first day of school, for instance, but recognise that the child must go to school. People who practise mindfulness find that their sense of empathy, or fellow feeling, becomes stronger over time. This tends to lead to an increasingly compassionate approach to other individuals.

In self-compassion, we treat ourselves with the compassion we might feel for others in similar circumstances. That includes not demanding perfection of ourselves. It includes recognising that the self arose from all sorts of causes, some of which may have been chosen, but many of which came about from random, accidental events. All of that being so, self-compassion is needed. None of us gets to shape ourselves perfectly. Moreover, nobody has ever been able to prove that perfection exists, except as an aspiration in our own minds.

So the cultivation of compassion towards oneself – that person in the mirror, who isn't in fact a failure – and towards others really matters. Self-compassion combats perfectionism so long as you are willing to have compassion for yourself without demanding perfection as the price.

Note that compassion for others also means that we accept their imperfections; we accept their faults. Such an acceptance towards the faults of others will rub off on ourselves. That's because, very often, what we condemn in others are the faults we possess but don't wish to admit.

The imperfection of mindfulness: It's worth noting that our mindfulness is always imperfect because our effort to be mindful always fails. This is because the natural behaviour of the brain is to wander into the past and the future. The brain gets lost in the forest of the imagination countless times a day. When we accept this, and when we call our attention back from its wandering without criticism, we are accepting our own imperfection. So if you are a perfectionist, be warned: the practice of mindfulness just might cure you of your affliction!

TRY THESE

Here are some mindfulness techniques that can help lift the curse of perfectionism.

Spot imperfections without criticism. The old Chinese Taoist philosophers valued imperfection and you could do worse than take a leaf out of their book. To do this, look out for imperfections – in objects, for instance: the chip on a vase, that scratch on George's furniture that I mentioned earlier, the picture that is very slightly askew. Look at them mindfully, perhaps with an awareness of your breath in the background, without criticising them in your head. This exericise can help you develop a tolerance for the inevitable imperfections of living.

Consider yourself 'always in beta'. See the work you send out into the world as 'always under review' or 'always in beta'. You are probably familiar with the fact that software programs tend to be issued 'in beta'. This means that while they are capable of performing the tasks they were intended for, there's still always room for tweaking – room for improvement. The improved software will be, of course, need improving itself before long, so in reality it's 'always in beta'. In seeing your work as 'always in beta', you acknowledge that the finished product may require tweaking – but first you get the finished product finished: tweaking, usually, can come later. Remember, though, that striving to make that work better does not mean striving for perfection – because perfection does not exist.

○ QUICK THOUGHT: Mindfully accept what is 'good enough' to free yourself from the straitjacket of perfectionism.

GET DOTTY

Practice: Use coloured, self-adhesive dots to bring you out of your worries and into mindful awareness.

Commentary: Because our attention naturally drifts away, you will often forget to be mindful. Those coloured paper dots you can buy in stationery departments can help with this. For instance, you might stick a dot on your keyboard. Whenever you see it, the dot will bring you back to the present moment.

Tips: I find placing a dot on a door handle I use a lot is effective. Putting a dot on the face of your watch will also remind you to be mindful whenever you look at it. Have an explanation ready for nosy people who want to know why you've got a dot there. 'It reminds me to be mindful' works for me. Remember to change the colour or the location every few days so you don't become so used to it that you stop noticing.

WHAT MIGHT WORK: DROP PRECISION IN MOST THINGS

My local supermarket has a bread bin and at the end of each day the bin is filled with loaves of bread, which are sold at a discount. I once spotted a man standing at the bin, picking up one loaf after another, examining them and then putting them back again.

When I had finished my shopping, I noticed that the man was still there, still going through loaves, judging them and putting them down again. His search for the 'right' loaf was not going well. Leaving aside the question of hygiene, I think we can assume that this man had a serious anxiety problem, and just couldn't stop searching.

But we can also admit, I think, that many of us have a mild version of whatever was troubling him.

THE SEARCH FOR THE 'RIGHT' ANSWER

We go on searching for the 'right' answer long after we have found an answer that might work and that would, in fact, be good enough. We worry about whether we have got the right answer. We think ourselves into a ball of tension about it.

Alternatively, we may just give up. Some research suggests that when faced with a wide range of choices, we sometimes give up and walk away without choosing anything at all. For instance, you might decide to watch a movie and find that after scrolling through the hundreds of choices available, you give up.

Now, that isn't something that should create a worry problem for us. But if, say, you had to choose a day for a company sales event, you could do exactly the same thing the man at the bread bin was doing: first there's the question of which week, which day, which time. If you can see relatively little to choose between them, you could easily get caught into a loop of worry and end up putting off a decision. You could have chosen by tossing a coin for all the difference it makes, but anxiety 'locked' you into going around and around in circles until you gave up. Meanwhile, you have solved nothing.

When's the right time to look for a raise? What should you get your girlfriend for Christmas? The list of choices about which you can agonise and obsess is a very long one indeed.

TRY THESE

Here are two ways that mindfulness can help with this. Please note that I don't have the perfect answer because I'm not looking for it!

Recognise the worry loop as an unhelpful reaction. Endless worry isn't really about the choices themselves but about the anxiety that making a choice conjures for you. The roots of this anxiety may lie hidden in childhood experiences and you may never unearth them. However, once you have recognised the issue in these terms, you can begin to deal with it. You will get caught into the loop now and then; however, the more you practise mindfulness, the more quickly you will recognise this when it happens. Then you can pull out of it. You can help yourself to pull out of it by noticing the tension in your body and observing it calmly. As you do this, you will begin to relax.

Look for what 'might' work. More often than not, you will find that the 'might work' solution will get the job done. Of course, I am not talking here about work that needs precision by its very nature. If you are engaged in landing an airliner, say, or in heart surgery, 'might work' won't do. I am talking here about the other 99 per cent (by my estimate) of human endeavour, in which precision is not essential. Going to Movie B 'might work' just as well as going to Movie A, for instance. Quite often, flipping a coin will produce just as good a result as all that thinking and analysis. What a humbling thought!

◯ QUICK THOUGHT: What 'might work' is usually better than the perfect solution you never manage to find.

GET YOUR SUMS WRONG

Practice: If you worry too much about getting everything right all the time, write $2+2=4$ across the top of a page, then cross out the 4.

Commentary: Among the most pointless sources of worry is the search for the perfect answer. In mathematics, $2+2=4$. In real life, $2+2$ might not equal 4 at all (there isn't a perfect way to hug someone you love, for instance). Sometimes precision matters, for instance in engineering (or reversing into a tight parking spot!). But very often, 'there or thereabouts' is both as good as it gets and good enough – and in those situations, there really is no merit in worrying about finding the 'right' answer.

Tips: Writing $2+2=4$ and then crossing out the 4 may seem silly. But it's there to remind you that sometimes it makes no significant difference if a decision is almost right instead of definitely right. Writing it will also remind you to bring your attention back to your posture or your breath or to do something else in the 'real' world when you find you've wandered off into your worries.

IMPERMANENCE: THE GOOD NEWS IS, EVERYTHING CHANGES

When Margaret's team brought in a big contract at work, she felt she was now on the fast track to the top. She spent the next weekend trying to come up with another big prospect. She had tasted victory and she never wanted to lose it again. And she wanted the firm to go on seeing her as a winner. A week later, she was worrying because she had failed to identify a new big fish to land. Then the team lost a medium-size contract and her mood went down and down. She became miserable. She felt as though she would never feel good again. And then she spent a weekend worrying about what would happen if the firm saw her as a loser.

Margaret was a victim of what I call 'the myth of the eternal moment'. This is the myth that the way you're feeling now is the way you're always going to feel. The way things are now is the way they are always going to be. It's an irrational belief but we all suffer from it. It brings us grief by making situations seem far more serious than they usually are.

Suppose you and your friends are going for dinner tomorrow night. You've been given the job of organising the restaurant and figuring out how to get there and how to get home. Your basic instruction is that your friends want to have a nice meal but they don't want to spend too much on it.

You begin to worry. What if the restaurant you've picked is the wrong one? What if the meal costs too much? What if your friends come to see you as a person who can't even arrange to book a table in a restaurant?

See what's happening? Somewhere in your brain is a voice telling you that if you get this thing wrong, you will be doomed for ever. Never again will anybody trust you to organise even a simple dinner date. You will have exposed your weaknesses as a social events organiser. Your friends will go into mourning at having had such an awful evening. Your reputation will be ruined for ever. You will live the rest of your days under a black cloud of failure and disapproval.

NOTHING IS FOR EVER

As you read this, you can see how silly it all is. In fact, you can see it is almost funny. But admit it: when you're looking at the possibility of something going wrong, at the back of your mind is the fear that it will go wrong for ever.

But actually, nothing is for ever. Things change. Let's

suppose that the restaurant turns out to be an even worse disaster than you feared it would be: rude waiters, slow service, high prices, inedible food. Then it takes an hour to get a taxi home. And somebody leaves their phone in the restaurant and it takes an hour to go back for it and then an hour to get home again. Not fun.

And yet the fact is that within days it will all have been largely forgotten. Within a month it will definitively be forgotten. Now and then the story may be told for a laugh at your expense and in fact you may even be one of those laughing. Once again, the myth of the eternal moment has been exposed for what it is – namely, a myth.

One of the cornerstones of Buddhist philosophy, from which mindfulness is derived, is the idea that everything is impermanent. On one level, that's stating the very obvious. But the very obvious needs to be stated again and again because of our habit of forgetting about it.

If you're feeling anxious right now, your anxiety is probably going to be gone as soon as whatever you're anxious about is done with. In fact, your anxiety may vanish in just a few minutes because you'll get distracted by something else. If you're facing an ordeal such as, let's say, giving a speech at a wedding, the anxiety attached to that will disappear when you've given the speech.

If you woke up this morning with a vague feeling of anxiety, you probably found that the feeling disappeared after a time.

KEY POINTS

Here are some key points relating to impermanence and mindfulness and how this can help us to worry less.

Your worries are impermanent

Worries are curious things. When we dwell on them they seem so real and so important. But what if I were to ask you to write down the five things you were worrying about this day last year? You probably wouldn't have a clue. And this day five years ago? Worries are impermanent. Most of last year's worries were replaced by this year's worries. Most of this year's worries will be replaced by next year's worries. Realising you will have forgotten most of today's worries by this time next year will help you to stop taking them so seriously.

Satisfaction is impermanent

If something is going well right now, you can be sure it's going to develop a kink or a little fault at some time in the future. How can that possibly be a comforting thought? Because when you accept the impermanence of everything, you needn't worry that what's going well now could go wrong in the future. You already know things will change, go wrong, break down, go out of date and so on. If you need to do something about some of that, fine, do it. But don't drive yourself crazy trying to hold off the inevitable.

Challenges
are impermanent too

Remember all those times you struggled with a new computer program? It seemed as though you would never master it. In fact, it seemed as though it was specifically designed to frustrate you and to take your happiness away for ever. Then eventually you 'got' it and today would probably be hard put to it to remember the experience. So your dissatisfaction was impermanent. Something or other will always be dissatisfying – but almost all dissatisfactions pass by in their own time and that's what's important to remember.

The psychological trait of habituation
is on your side

One of the most interesting aspects of our approach to change in life is that, in fact, we can get used to anything. This is called habituation. It's why if you won the lottery, you would get used to having all those millions sooner than you think (which doesn't mean I wouldn't like to win the lottery). It's why people with chronic conditions become used to them and can pick up many of the threads of their lives again. Change often seems scary before it happens and we can indulge in a great deal of unnecessary worry about it – but, more often than you might think, not too long after the change happens we see nothing remarkable about it. This isn't to deny that some changes aren't life-changing in bad as well as good ways. But most changes become humdrum after we have experienced them for a while.

TRY THESE

Here are some ways you can put what you have learned here into practice.

Practise awareness of the present moment. The practice of awareness of the present moment by coming into that awareness often during the day makes us more comfortable with impermanence. We know by observation that every moment is different. By bringing a calm awareness to the changing moments, we bring a calm awareness to our changing lives. Instead of resisting the inevitable, allow yourself to become calmly aware of it. You no longer follow your mind as it resists change with thoughts and fantasies but instead return calmly to what's going on right now.

Remember, 'this too will pass'. This traditional saying sums up this chapter. Unless you suffer from a generalised anxiety disorder (see the chapter 'Extreme anxiety: Panic attacks and other conditions', page 107), your anxiety will sooner or later pass – and even extreme anxiety changes in intensity and is sometimes absent. That's so long as you don't keep it alive by worrying about it when you could be doing something useful instead. Remember that phrase and call it to mind whenever you find yourself caught up in the myth of the eternal moment.

○ QUICK THOUGHT: Accepting that nothing is permanent can bring you more peace of mind than resisting the inevitability of change.

NOTICE THE CHAIR

Practice: Next time you're sitting in a chair, notice the feeling of your back against the back of the chair and of your feet against the soles of your shoes.

Commentary: Most of us spend a lot of our time sitting down, usually at desks, staring into screens. Very often, that's where we do our worrying. This exercise provides an opportunity to replace worry with mindfulness practice. The key is to make mindfulness a habitual practice, not just something you do when you worry. Every now and then, whenever a phone rings for instance, bring your awareness to that feeling of your back against a chair or your feet against the soles of your shoes.

Tips: Try also to notice a sense of stillness in your body and to stay with your awareness of that stillness for a little while. You may find that stillness between your ribcage and your tummy.

PART SIX: THE STRESS EFFECT: OUR BODIES AND OTHER BODIES

GETTING INTO YOUR GENES: WHY DE-STRESSING MATTERS

Jack believes that all this talk about stress is nonsense made up by doctors and by people like me to make money out of him. His wife Geraldine shares his belief. As far as she is concerned, what you do when you meet adversity is get on with it and quit whining about stress. They are both so entirely sure that they are right about this that they go around under the impression that everybody thinks they are right about everything. But they are not right. Even people who have no time for all this 'emotional nonsense' need to know about the effects of stress on the body. One of the most serious aspects of stress, which might even impress Jack and Geraldine, is that it can affect your genes and contribute to earlier ageing.

INTRODUCING TELOMERES

One of the most important discoveries in the field of stress has been the link between stress and cell ageing. As you probably know, the DNA within our cells contains the instructions for the creation of those cells. Those instructions come in sets of genes that are strung together. The sets are called chromosomes. Our genes are susceptible to damage and so they have to be protected. The chromosomes need protection also. Think of all the instructions that make you up – as you are made up of your cells – as packets of chromosomes all linked together. Between the chromosomes are buffers called telomeres. The telomeres protect the chromosomes and in that way protect the cells of your body. But as time goes on, they wear and tear. For instance, every time a cell splits and duplicates itself, you lose a little telomere in the process. This eventually leads to cell damage, cell death and ageing. So those telomeres are really, really important. If Jack and Geraldine want to retain their youthful looks, they had better take care of them. One of the ways to take care of them is to lower your levels of stress.

Stress affects those telomeres negatively. They become shorter and that's bad for them. Children subjected to extremely stressful situations when they are small have shorter telomeres and are more susceptible to stress later in life. We also know that older carers can end up with shorter telomeres, which accelerate ageing, because of the stressful nature of their task.

This is not meant to frighten you. It is meant to make the point that no matter what your stage of life, to lower your levels of stress can be a great investment in your future. If you're a person who is so used to stress that it feels like it has become part of who you are, stress reduction is really valuable.

Stress doesn't just shorten your telomeres, it also tends to reduce your ability to resist impulses, and it makes your brain more sensitive to rewards. This can increase the attractiveness of comfort eating, comfort drinking and other escapist behaviours. If you have any addictions, or if you're in any way susceptible to addiction, then stress can push you deeper into the addiction zone.

Talking of comfort eating, your body also puts on fat as a response to stress. Stress tells the cells in your abdomen that store fat to switch on and start putting fat away, and comfort eating means more fat to put into those cells.

As you can see, reducing your stress levels is quite a big deal.

TRY THESE

Here are two very practical ways to protect yourself against stress and keep those telomeres in good shape.

Exercise. Exercise is one of the great protectors against stress. People who practise mindfulness are less likely to sit around being couch potatoes, lost in their thoughts or in television or in a game. In his work at Oxford University on mindfulness and depression, Professor Mark Williams found that people who are mindful are more active (for more on his work, see the Resources chapter, page 220). When you are not lost and wandering in your mind, you are more likely to get up and do something.

Nourish your social connections. A big protector against stress and its effects is a good, functioning social network. This doesn't mean that your home has to be full all the time with friends, it just means keeping in touch with people – this could be by phone, by text, by email or in other ways in addition to meeting people. Mindfulness tends to increase activity in the insula, a part of the brain involved in feelings of empathy. In other words, mindful people tend to be more empathic. That in itself encourages those who are mindful to develop their networks and take care of them.

Only our thoughts: Bear in mind also that mindfulness itself can be hugely beneficial in lowering stress. Dr Elissa Epel – one of the people on whose work I have drawn for this chapter – of the University of California is a practitioner of mindfulness. She says of chronic stress (in an interview with the American Psychological Association's Monitor on Psychology) that 'viewed mindfully, no situation is truly chronic – there are always calm moments to notice and be present for.'

○ QUICK THOUGHT: Time and effort put into lowering stress is hugely beneficial and can protect the health of the very cells of which your body is made.

OUT THE DOOR

Practice: Place a reminder by the door to bring you into mindfulness when you leave your home.

Commentary: Getting out the door can be a frantic activity, especially in the mornings. You're late for work, the dog wants a walk, the kids are acting up -- mindlessness is the order of the moment. Placing a reminder inside the door to recall you to mindfulness can make a difference to the quality of your day. And if you don't have kids, dogs etc. to get you agitated, that reminder could help you to leave the building mindfully and not lost in a loop of worry.

Tips: A tall vase of flowers (even good artificial flowers), a picture, a card, a self-adhesive dot are all examples of objects you can use as a mindfulness reminder. If you have kids, consider putting them in charge of coming up with a reminder – that way, they will remind you to be mindful if they notice you're not paying attention! You could also designate something outside the door – a tree, a postbox, a hill or building in the distance – as your reminder.

ANXIOUS BODIES: IT ISN'T ALL IN THE MIND

'It's all in the mind, isn't it?' That's what a woman who suffered from anxiety once said to me. When I told her that anxiety was in the body as much as in the mind, and maybe more so, she looked at me as though I had two heads. But as she had told me about the anxiety in her mind, anyone looking at her could have spotted the anxiety in her body: her raised shoulders, her furrowed brow, her pursed lips – they all told the story. Moreover, she had looked like this for as long as I had known her. Indeed, some people found her difficult to approach, misinterpreting her anxiety as hostility.

It's important and helpful to remember that anxiety isn't all in the mind. It could even be argued that the mind is less important than the body in our 'felt' experience of anxiety.

FIGHT OR FLIGHT?

When your brain thinks you are in any kind of danger, it immediately sends out messages to get you ready to fight that danger or to flee. Adrenalin begins to flow through your system, for instance, and alters the flow of blood to protect your inner organs. It's only after all this has started happening that you get to find out about it at a conscious level.

Suddenly you feel anxious – but that feeling has come into your awareness rather late in the chain of reactions. Why? Because your body wants to get you to start taking action to remove you from danger without having to wait around while you think about it. That's why it gets you into 'fight or flight' mode so quickly that it's happened before you know about it.

But, you might say, I'm not actually in danger most of the time when I feel anxious or when I find myself worrying. That's true, but the systems involved in worry, anxiety and stress are very old systems. They date from prehistoric times, when our business was survival. In many respects, they operate today as they did when survival for most people was a more precarious affair.

The important point is not that these reactions occur to keep us safe even when we don't need to be kept safe. What really matters is that anxiety and stress are very physical experiences and, by calming the body, mindful practice can calm our anxious, worrying selves.

TRY THESE

Here are two ways to calm your emotions by taking your awareness to your body.

Observe your body relaxing. You can do this on the train, at home, or if you're sitting or lying down in a park. Allow your body to relax and observe this happening as it occurs. This requires awareness and attention and it can be helped along by allowing your breath to slow down. Simply observing your breath will slow it down. Because your emotions are made up of thoughts, feelings and physical sensations, this practice will calm your emotions as well as your body.

Move from thought to sensation. It can be difficult, some would say impossible, to focus on thought and on a physical sensation at the same time. To take advantage of this, if you find yourself worrying and thinking anxious thoughts, practise shifting your attention to your body. Allow your attention to rest on the physical sensations. As you do this, you could also maintain a background awareness of your breathing. After a time, you will probably notice a shift in the overall sense of anxiety, because physical sensations change over time. You could then move gradually into a wider awareness of your whole body, maintaining that awareness for a while.

Freedom from anxious thoughts: The woman I mentioned at the start of this chapter found relaxing into her body particularly helpful. She especially enjoyed the freedom of not having to think anxious thoughts. This was the first time she had realised that she was not under some sort of obligation to worry. She also needed help from a therapist to deal with some of the childhood issues that had led to her experiencing this degree of anxiety. However, she found that practising mindfulness of the body brought about a huge improvement.

QUICK THOUGHT: Worry and anxiety can occur in your body as well as in your thoughts and by calming your body, you can calm worry and anxiety.

STAY IN YOUR BODY

Practice: Maintain at least some awareness of your body as you go through your day.

Commentary: Staying in your body is a great way to maintain awareness and presence of mind. When you are lost in worry, it's as though your body doesn't exist; only the thoughts in your head seem real. Your body may as well have floated off somewhere on its own! Awareness of the body is an old and effective mindfulness practice, dating back more than two millennia.

Tips: When you are standing up from a seat or sitting down into it, be aware of the physical sensations. When you are standing in line, bring your attention to your body, for instance to the sensations in your feet. Now and then, pause and become aware of the sensations in your entire body.

FAMILIES: LIVING WITH 'INHERITED' ANXIETY

Harry approached me after a workshop one day to tell me that he had always had high levels of worry and anxiety. He had never succeeded in finding a way to get rid of it and he found the battle against anxiety exhausting.

I asked Harry how far back he could remember his anxiety going. All the way back to childhood, he replied. He recalled worrying whether Santa would turn up on Christmas Day (he always did), and whether the teachers liked or disliked him at school. As he got older, he worried about exams, girls and friendships, as most teenagers do.

Did other people in the house worry like that? I asked. Oh yes, he said. His parents were champions when it came to anxiety. Even as kids, Harry and his sister had known about the bills they worried about paying and about their father's health concerns – he was a bit of a hypochondriac, it seems. They also worried constantly about what the neighbours thought of them.

WAYS TO CREATE A
PREDISPOSITION TO ANXIETY

Anxiety and worry, in other words, were the lenses through which Harry's family approached the world. And this is a common way in which parents can give their children a predisposition to anxiety. The child knows of no other way of looking at life except through the lens that their parents provide.

It's not the only way in which families create worry and anxiety. Elsewhere, you'll find mention of the curse of perfectionism (see 'Always in beta: Lifting the curse of perfectionism', page 125). Perfectionism results in excessive demands that we place on ourselves and that we can never really meet. This faulty demand on the self can originate from parents' demands that the child should perform to impossible expectations. While growing up, the child feels judged and can never quite win the approval of the parents – or can only get that approval for behaviours that the parents deem 'perfect'. This develops into anxiety. The person may be anxious that they are not measuring up at work, regardless of the quality of what they do. Or they may see themselves as an inadequate parent, despite being loving and nurturing to their children.

The third way in which families can create anxiety and stress is through a genetic inheritance. The innumerable instructions in our DNA that contribute to our personalities have many, many variations. Some of these variations may make a person more susceptible to anxiety, especially in circumstances that provoke high levels of stress, such as moving house or separating from a partner.

Researchers also suggest that children who are subjected to serious stress at a very early age can be overreactive to stress later in life. If you are one such person, it's especially beneficial to practise mindfulness, so that you do not make your stress levels greater than they need to be. It isn't that you are doomed to be overstressed for the rest of your life, but rather that you need to take an active role in managing your stress so that you keep it as low as you can. All the mindfulness techniques you've read about in this book will help you to do that.

And if, as parents, we are able to create a reasonably low-stress environment for our children, they will benefit throughout their lives. This does not mean that you have to pamper them or treat them like princes and princesses. It simply means trying to provide an environment that doesn't have extreme levels of stress.

Teaching children some little ways to de-stress themselves can also give them skills to carry through life. For instance, you could all have quiet moments when you sit down and focus gently on your breathing for a couple of minutes once or twice a day.

HOW MINDFULNESS CAN HELP

Since families can pass on high stress levels and a tendency to worry, we can see that some of us will always be somewhat more anxious than others. In that case, what is the point in bothering with mindfulness, you might ask?

Well, mindfulness can still help you to achieve significant reductions in anxiety. Mindfulness affects physical structures in the brain in ways that make you less reactive to negative thoughts. For instance, the amygdala, the alarm system of the brain, becomes smaller and quieter in people who practise mindfulness consistently.

If you have suffered chronic anxiety and chronic worrying for years, a fall in general levels of anxiety and any drop in the degree of worrying can come as a huge relief. By practising mindfulness you can experience that relief, and become aware that it is possible to go through life with lower levels of anxiety, worry and stress. And the more you practise mindfulness, the more liberated you will feel from the disabling effects of severe anxiety and worry.

An especially helpful practice if you have inherited high anxiety from your family – genetically or otherwise – is the body scan. It's a good mindfulness practice at any time, but especially at night when you want to sleep. One of the more debilitating aspects of high levels of anxiety is that it can lead you to stay awake at night. You toss and turn, worrying uselessly about present, past and future, and then crawl through the next day in a state of exhaustion. You will have found out the hard way that worrying in the middle of the night is almost always entirely pointless. Instead, do a body scan, moving your attention from your toes up to the top of your head slowly and in detail (see 'Slow body scan', page 17). Whenever your mind returns to anxious thoughts as you do this, bring your attention back to the body scan.

Mindfulness also helps greatly by encouraging us to accept those levels of anxiety that are inevitable. You may recall that Harry mentioned finding the fight against anxiety draining. This in itself had demoralised him. In mindfulness, however, you sidestep that exhausting battle. You do so by accepting that anxiety and worry come with life. If you're a very anxious person, then acceptance, a core aspect of mindfulness, might just be your best friend.

TRY THESE

Here are two more mindfulness practices you could use if you have inherited high levels of anxiety from your family.

Practise mindfulness of the out-breath. The out-breath engages that part of the central nervous system that calms you down. For that reason, spending time now and then placing your attention on your out-breath can be an excellent way to lower your levels of anxiety. This is very easy to do. Sit for a few minutes now and then and observe your out-breath without forcing it. Follow the breath all the way out. Allow yourself to breathe in easily and calmly. Then follow your out-breath again.

Practise belly-breathing. As you know if you are a particularly anxious person, we often feel our anxiety in our tummies. Sitting and calmly observing your tummy as you breathe can be a great way to get your head out of your worries. Begin by noticing how your tummy moves in and out as you breathe. After a while, notice how your lower back also moves in and out as you breathe, though much more subtly than your tummy. Now put your attention on your entire tummy and lower back as you breathe. Every time you drift back into worrying, gently bring your attention back to your tummy. Even if you only do this for a few minutes a couple of times a day, you will find that this practice will help to calm you. As a bonus, remember that you can't focus on your tummy and worry at the same time.

○ QUICK THOUGHT: Some people have higher than usual levels of anxiety for genetic and other family-based reasons and can gain a great deal of relief from the practice of mindfulness.

BREATHE THROUGH THE FLOOR

Practice: Rest your attention on your out-breath and allow it to flow all the way out, as if going down through the floor.

Commentary: The out-breath engages that part of the nervous system that calms you. Therefore, attending to your out-breath is helpful if you are agitated or you are trying to get back to sleep at night. You don't have to push the breath out – allow your attention to rest on the experience. At night, especially, the out-breath can seem to go on for a long time as you sink into it and, sometimes, into sleep.

Tips: Notice the sensations in your body as the out-breath occurs. Notice the subtle changes in the breath from beginning to end. Then notice the tiny, tiny pause before you breathe in again. This is probably easier to practise if you put a little quiet time aside for it.

RELATIONSHIPS: CHALLENGE
ASSUMPTIONS TO CUT STRESS

When Gilbert and Annabel fight, they stop talking to each other for weeks afterwards. The atmosphere in the house becomes oppressive, as their children can attest to. Over the years, each explained to their children that the other needed to admit that he or she was wrong before normal relations could be resumed. In the opinion of each, the other person was wrong to fight in the first place, let alone engage in whatever disagreement led to the fight. Fighting is just not acceptable, they would explain.

Annabel's parents used to visit every few weeks and that usually brought hostilities to a close. Neither Gilbert nor Annabel wanted the parents to know that they had been living in sulky silence. Soon, the children began tipping off their grandparents, to prompt a visit; it had not taken them long to figure out that this was the only way to get their parents talking to each other again. Years later, the children left for university and their grandparents moved to Spain. Gilbert and Annabel are now left to endure ever lengthier silences.

Gilbert and Annabel are trying to control each other. If they can't do it through fighting, they each try to do it through silence. They have failed to realise that, except in extreme situations, you cannot control another person in a relationship. The other person may choose to go along with what you want, but that's not the same thing as being controlled. They also fail to appreciate the importance of acceptance in long-term relationships. No long-term relationship could survive in any sort of satisfactory way without acceptance of each other's faults.

Mindfulness could help Gilbert and Annabel. Mindful awareness enables us to step out of habitual patterns of thinking. In particular, it gives us the opportunity to spot unhelpful patterns and assumptions in our relationships. By patterns, I mean ways of thinking, seeing and behaving that are so familiar we hardly notice them any more – yet they have a strong influence on our experience of living and on that of those around us. Gilbert and Annabel can become mindful of the triggers (a remark, a look, for instance) that start them off on yet another conflict. Having learned to spot their triggers, they can then learn to respond without fighting, if they sincerely want to stop fighting.

HARMFUL ASSUMPTIONS AND HOW MINDFULNESS CAN HELP

Let's look at some patterns and unexamined assumptions that bring anxiety to relationships and at how mindfulness can help with these.

People in close relationships should never fight

This is a remarkable assumption, given that people in long-term relationships do fight and thereby prove it wrong in the process. Yet many hold on to the irrational belief that people in close relationships should never fight, and for that reason they see a fight in itself as a terrible thing and more important than it really is. Some research suggests that people who enter a marriage with this belief are more likely to divorce! When people enter a long-term relationship, a point comes when the other person's habits and behaviours seem more irritating than they did at the start. This is the 'why can't you be more like me' phase. To get through this phase, people need to accept each other's differences. Each, no doubt, will try to influence the other and may even have some success, but differences will remain nonetheless. Mindful acceptance is an essential survival tool in this sort of situation, as is a sense of humour.

If we fight, I must keep rerunning
it through my mind

Some people are good at getting over fights. The sparks fly, and then it's finished and done with. But others keep the fight going on in their head for days, or even weeks, afterwards. It is as though they feel they owe it to themselves to keep the reruns rolling: what he did, what she said, what he didn't do, what she didn't say. These reruns, usually accompanied by silence, generally poison the atmosphere and make everyone feel wretched. They achieve nothing. In a healthy relationship, people bounce back faster. During the fight, the other person was the worst, the most inconsiderate human being of all time, but when the emotions cool down, these distorted assumptions cool with them. Usually the fight is allowed to drift into the past.

But that can only happen if both parties drop that brooding. Brooding keeps the hostilities alive. Mindfulness helps people in this regard because it discourages brooding. You find yourself in the middle of a mental rerun and you stop the movie and come out into the clear light of the present moment. So mindfulness can contribute a great deal to the peace of mind of partners over a long number of years.

You must live up to my expectations or I must live up to yours

This demand can blight the relationship between parents and teenage children in particular (though it can harm relationships between older people, too). Parents must help their children to become social beings and this involves an insistence that the child behaves in certain basic ways. That insistence works far more effectively when the child is young and before the teenage years begin. But if the weight of expectation is too heavy – for instance, if the parents demand perfection or insist that the child takes up a certain career – then conflict is likely to follow. Parents need to accept that each child has his or her own personality and preferences. With that acceptance, the parent can hope to influence the child for his or her own good without wasting energy in unjustifiable battles, and in the knowledge that the child may take a different path.

Mindful acceptance makes it easier to create that space in which the child can flourish. And part of the acceptance needs to be that fights will happen. It's part of a process in which we inevitably rub up against each other in the wrong way.

I must know what you are thinking and you must know what I am thinking

'If you loved me, you would know what I was thinking' is an assumption that brings conflict into many partnerships.

So can the assumption that 'because I love you, I know what you are thinking'. In psychology, particularly in Cognitive Behavioural Therapy, mind-reading is seen as a major distortion. We need to understand that people in a relationship remain individual, no matter how close that relationship may be. Their minds and thoughts remain individual minds and thoughts. Acceptance of this is a major step forward in creating a harmonious relationship. It helps that mindfulness is a great deal less concerned with what we are thinking than with what's actually happening in reality.

Everything is all right no matter what and if something seems wrong then I just have to put up with it

Sometimes we fool ourselves into thinking that everything is all right even though a loved one is treating us badly. So, for example, if the other person treats us with contempt, we may tell ourselves that it is our fault, or that they are just a little short-tempered. But maybe it isn't our fault and maybe it's not enough to excuse the behaviour as a display of short temper.

If I am being mindful, bringing my attention continually back to the present moment, then I will find it harder to deceive myself into thinking everything is my fault. How does acceptance come into this? Perhaps I need to accept that all is not well. Perhaps I need to accept also that I deserve to be treated better. If I accept these things, then I am more likely to seek change, to change my own reactions, or even to leave the relationship.

Suppose your adult children bully you, demanding that you be a source of income while also acting as chef and general servant. You need to be able to accept that these are no longer the nice children you once brought up and remind yourself that you deserve respect. When you accept this, you are more ready to demand proper treatment from your children. At the very least, you might decide to stop acting as unpaid cook and butler. Sometimes, mindful acceptance is not about peace and light; sometimes it is about facing the harsh realities of a situation and seeking the change that you need.

I should make it clear that none of what I have written above constitutes a suggestion that anyone should stay in an emotionally or physically abusive relationship. What I am dealing with here are normal patterns of conflict in relationships.

TRY THIS

Here are two mindfulness practices that can help in long-term relationships.

Naikan

This is a Japanese practice, which can give us a fresh review of our relationships and which I have adapted slightly. To do this, think of somebody who means a good deal to you and then ask yourself three questions.

1. What has this person given me?

2. What have I given this person?

3. What else has this person given me?

Give some detailed, specific answers to the questions.

Let's say the person is your mother.

What has this person given me? Your mother got you out to school in the mornings, fed you, took you to the doctor when you were sick, and so on.

What have I given this person? Think of specific details like remembering her birthday, decorating the house for her, taking her out to lunch.

What else has this person given me? Perhaps she gave up or interrupted her career to care for you. Perhaps she took you in when you lost your flat and your job. Maybe she now babysits your children.

Try Naikan also about your partner, your wife, your children, in fact anybody who is important to you. Asking the third question makes you dig deeper than you might ordinarily do. It can rebalance your attitude towards the relationship and towards yourself: you can see that you have not only received but given and not only given but received.

By the way, you can do Naikan not only on people you've disagreed with but on anybody of significance in your life.

Wishing well

This is an adaptation of an old Buddhist practice called 'loving kindness', and can be applied to anyone you are close to. It can be especially helpful if you are at logger-heads with them.

First, call to mind the person whom you want to wish well. Imagine that this person is sitting before you, but imagine them at a time when you were feeling good about each other. That might have been a month ago, a year ago or an hour ago. Say silently to the person, 'May you be happy, may you be well.' If you don't like that language, you could change it to something like: 'Be happy, be well.' Say this a few times and really try to feel it and to mean it. Now imagine the person as they are right now, as though they are sitting in front of you. Once again, say, 'May you be happy, may you be well.' Try to really feel that sense of well-wishing. Wish them well a few times. See if you feel any different now.

You could apply this practice to anyone and in the original Buddhist version you would include yourself (wishing well to yourself), a friend, a person you don't know well and a person you disliked. The version here is aimed at helping your relationship with someone with whom you usually get on reasonably well but with whom you may also fall out from time to time.

○ QUICK THOUGHT: Mindful acceptance can make an enormous contribution to the quality of your relationships.

PART SEVEN: A NEW RELATIONSHIP WITH WORRY, STRESS AND ANXIETY

GOING WRONG: PESSIMISM
AS AN ASSET

Peter worked with me on a variety of projects some years ago. I was always struck by the fact that, though he handled quite big projects for sometimes difficult clients, he always strolled about looking relaxed. I once asked him what his secret was.

'I'm a pessimist,' he replied. It turned out that Peter made the simple assumption that whatever he worked on would go wrong in some small way. Armed with this knowledge, he did his best and then he relaxed. He did not demand perfection of himself because he knew that perfection is, really, a fantasy. And he didn't go around in a ball of anxiety wondering if something *might* go wrong because he already knew something *would* go wrong. This approach made him really good at doing what was in his control to do, and his projects satisfied even easily dissatisfied clients.

When you imagine a person who assumes that everything is going to go wrong in some way, you don't think of

Peter – you think of someone negative. You think of someone with their own personal black cloud, one that follows them around while they worry their days away. Isn't this what pessimists are like? As Peter's story shows, not necessarily.

The person who can accept with equanimity that things go wrong and that nothing is perfect is set fair to take a relaxed approach to life. Instead of beating themselves up trying to get everything 100 per cent right, they do the best they can and leave the outcome to fate.

WORKING WITH DISSATISFACTION

This idea that something will always be a little out of kilter, a little dissatisfying, is a key principle of Buddhist psychology, which shaped the practice of mindfulness today.

You've probably heard it said that, according to the Buddhists, life is suffering. A more accurate translation might be that life always contains dissatisfactions. One of the wheels on your wagon – to use a Buddhist metaphor – will always have a wobble. Nothing is ever quite 100 per cent right and a lot of our happiness depends on being able to accept this fact.

Suppose you've planned a promotional event for your workplace or your business. Let's say you are worrying a lot about whether or not everything will turn out right. If you shift to a mindful perspective, you will accept that on the day something will not be *completely* right

– something will go wrong – and that's okay. What you want to ensure is that events run as smoothly as you can reasonably manage. Doing what you can to create the conditions for success by making your own best effort *is* within your control. What *isn't* within your control is the outcome – that's the part you need to be able to accept.

You can hold a garden party to promote your product but you can't dictate the weather. Neither can you dictate the traffic on the way to your party. But you can get in a marquee to protect guests from the rain. You can check with the police or the local council to see if road closures are planned that could slow traffic down. But when you have done as much as you can reasonably do, you need to bring your attention right into the present instead of sitting there worrying.

TRY THESE

Here are two specific ways to put into practice the acceptance that our efforts are never 100 per cent successful.

Draw a line. Make a list of tasks or issues you need to consider about your project. Then take a clean sheet of paper and divide the page into two columns. In the left-hand column, list the tasks or issues that are in your control; in the right-hand column, write down those that are outside your control. In the example above, the weather on the day is outside your control. What's inside your control is to hire a marquee or to place complimentary umbrellas around the garden. Continue that process until you have a complete list and then focus on the 'in my control' column. When you find yourself mulling over the event as the days go by, get into the habit of using two different phrases to help deal with that thinking; the phrases are 'in my control' and 'not in my control'. For instance, if you're worrying about how people might react to the speech you're giving, you might say to yourself the phrase 'not in my control'. That's because their reaction really isn't in your control. If you think about preparing the speech, you might say 'in my control', because how you prepare is very much in your control. This mindfulness practice takes a little work, but it is an excellent way, I think, to reduce worrying before an event and to do that worrying in a useful way.

Try a 5 per cent rule. Look at your event and ask yourself how it would be if 5 per cent of your preparations went wrong. Remember that's still only one in 20, and that's probably as much as is going to go wrong, unless you're about to have an extremely bad day indeed. Now think about that a little. Notice if you feel a little tense, physically, and observe that tension without comment until it goes. This will make it much easier for you to face the fact that something, however little, is likely to go wrong. In fact, if you can look at the possibilities calmly, you will be far more likely to be able to do something sensible about them.

○ QUICK THOUGHT: Accept that something will go wrong with whatever you're doing, figure out what is in your control to do about this, do it and relax.

BREATHE WITH TODAY'S DISSATISFACTIONS

Practice: If you know of an event coming up today that you dislike, notice how this affects your breathing and wait for your breath to become calm.

Commentary: Today is likely to include both what you like and what you don't like. In mindfulness, we drop the struggle with unavoidable realities that we dislike. The struggle is mainly carried out through complaining in our minds about whatever it is that we don't like. If you know of an effective action you can take to change what you don't like for the better, take it. Very often, we can't do much about the events we dislike, except complain to ourselves about the unfairness of it all. Noticing your breath and waiting for the breathing to become calm suspends that complaining in the mind. It also helps to calm you as you face the day's events.

Tips: As well as your breath, notice any tensing of your muscles that thinking about this event causes. Now wait for the tension to relax. At the same time, allow your breathing to calm.

MORITA THERAPY: MAKING PEACE WITH NERVOUSNESS

John wants to apply for promotion but whenever he sits down to write his application he begins to worry. Has he enough qualifications? What will his colleagues think of him if he gets promoted? What if his new responsibilities are beyond him? And so on and so on. After sitting there worrying like this for a while, he decides to put off filling in the application. Tomorrow or the day after tomorrow he will feel better about it, he assures himself. Gradually, he allows the deadline for the application to come and go without taking any action other than worrying. A simple approach, called the Morita Therapy, could have helped John to at least get his application in and to leave the worrying until later.

The Morita Therapy was developed a century ago by Japanese psychiatrist Dr Shoma Morita. His method could be summed up in three lines, as translated by psychologist Dr David K. Reynolds:

- Know your purpose.

- Know your feelings.

- Do what needs to be done.

HOW THE FORMULA WORKS

Sound simple? Yes, it does – and that's because it is. But though it's simple, it's by no means simplistic. Let's take a closer look at how this useful formula works.

Suppose your purpose is to deliver a speech to your colleagues at a company seminar. Naturally you want to put in an impressive performance. Trouble is, you feel extremely nervous. What if you fall flat on your face? What if you stumble over your words, get your facts wrong or generally make a fool of yourself?

Should you try to get out of it and generally avoid such challenges until you have sorted out your anxiety about public speaking? No. According to Dr Morita (and this is very much a mindfulness approach), you need to take two steps: (a) acknowledge that you are anxious, without dwelling on it (*know your feelings*) and (b) prepare your speech and then deliver it (*do what needs to be done*). So the full sequence is: you know you want to deliver a clear, effective speech *(purpose)*; acknowledge your anxiety *(feelings)*, prepare as best you can and make the speech *(what needs to be done)*.

Like many apparently simple ideas, this has a great deal

of wisdom in it. To wait for your feelings to change before you do what you need to do just doesn't work. Very often in life, you only get to feel good about actions after you have actually done them. If you wait for your feelings to change first, you may never get to move forward. People who don't understand this can stay stuck for a long time. They will put off tasks until they have conquered their feelings of nervousness, but conquering nervousness does not magically happen. That's human nature. You will find more on this in the next chapter on exposure ('Exposure: Experience fears to face them down', page 189).

Dr Morita's advice was both simple and wise. And to do what needs to be done while allowing your feelings to accompany you, so to speak, is a pure mindfulness approach.

I think Dr Morita's theory also underlines an important principle: our feelings are like the weather – they are outside our direct control. Otherwise we would (unless we were very odd people indeed) choose to be happy all the time! What's in our control is our behaviour. That's where we need to put the emphasis when we take a mindful approach to anxiety, worry and stress. We do what needs to be done to fulfil our purpose even though our feelings want to push us in another direction.

You might find a bonus here. Often, when we have done what needs to be done, our feelings of nervousness subside and to do it again becomes easier. But for all of this to work, we have to act without minds clouded by negative dramas. None of this, of course, is an invitation to act recklessly: do not go down that dark alley alone if your feelings tell you to stay away. But I think we are all able to make the distinction between feelings that are justified and those we simply need to acknowledge.

That acknowledgement matters because it's often an inability to tolerate our own feelings that stops us in our tracks (see the chapter 'Increase tolerance: You can't take it? Yes you can!', page 61). So next time you're faced with a task about which you feel nervous and from which you want to shrink back, remember the three steps. Remind yourself of your purpose, acknowledge your feelings and do what's needed to get on with the task.

TRY THESE

Here are two techniques that can help you bring Morita's ideas into your day.

Write it down. Write down 'Do what needs to be done' and keep it where you'll see it every now and then. For instance, you could write 'Do what needs to be done' as the subject line of an email and send it to yourself so that you will spot it whenever you look at your inbox. It might even remind you that checking your emails is not necessarily 'what needs to be done'!

Do the easiest thing. When you face a daunting project, pick the easiest task that needs doing and do it. Don't wait until you feel better about doing it – pick the task and get on with it. It has been said that difficult projects begin with easy steps – it might be looking up a website or making a phone call, for instance. By taking these easy steps instead of wandering off into lots of 'catastrophising' ideas, you become far more effective at moving forward.

○ QUICK THOUGHT: Know your purpose. Know your feelings. Do what needs to be done.

A MINDFUL TO-DO LIST

Practice: Look at your to-do list with awareness of your breathing and without escaping into fantasies or other activities.

Commentary: Glancing down your to-do list probably brings up all sorts of reactions you are not aware of. Muscles may tense, breath may shorten, shoulders may lift, you may even hunch over a little. These reactions can make you want to escape from the physical feelings they arouse. But once you are aware of what is going on, you can make a rational choice about what to do next. Otherwise, you may keep putting off tasks that are relatively simple and end up, yet again, in a stew at the eleventh hour.

Tips: As you glance down your list, observe your breath. If you notice your breathing tightening up a little, pause. Ask yourself what the smallest thing is that you could do to make progress on this task. Look up a phone number? Work on it for three minutes? Whatever you do, maintain a calm awareness of your breathing so that you increase your tolerance for tasks that make you feel tense.

EXPOSURE: EXPERIENCE FEARS
TO FACE THEM DOWN

Maureen once had a panic attack in a shopping centre. It came completely out of the blue, with no warning, and with no obvious cause. This is very often the case with panic attacks (see the chapter 'Extreme anxiety: Panic attacks and other conditions', page 107). Maureen now finds that her anxiety levels go through the roof if she walks into a shopping centre. In fact, she usually gets no further than the car park. This is very inconvenient for her because she lives beside the shopping centre but now has to travel at least two miles to go to an alternative store.

Over the decades, psychologists have found that exposure to what you fear is very often the only cure. For instance, if you have a fear of walking through shopping centres, a therapist might encourage you to go as far as the entrance, stay there for long enough to feel the fear, and then retreat. Next time, you might take a few steps inside with a friend until you have felt the fear for a while, and then allow yourself to leave again. Eventually, you might learn to walk through the whole shopping centre accompanied by your friend.

Later, when you're able to do all of that fairly easily, you might get your friend to wait inside the centre while you walk through alone. Through these gradual steps, you train your mind to drop the fear of walking through the shopping centre. This is the process of 'Exposure', and it is through this process that we can most often help ourselves to deal with this sort of anxiety.

If, instead, we stay at home worrying about it and then avoiding it, we get nowhere and we take no steps to help ourselves. Sometimes we make the mistake of saying 'I will do the thing I'm afraid of when I'm no longer afraid of it'. That won't work. It is only through doing it, through exposing yourself to it, that you will be able to lose that fear in the first place.

You have had many experiences that you first approached with worry, stress or anxiety and that now don't bother you at all. For some, the source of anxiety might have been speaking in front of a group of people, or driving, or even walking down the street. But constant exposure to it gradually quietened the alarm bells. Now you might even wonder what all the fuss was about; now you might even enjoy it.

MINDFUL EXPOSURE AND EQUANIMITY

What does all this have to do with mindfulness? If you think about mindfulness for a moment, you will see that it is actually a form of exposure to our experiences. We don't escape into our imagination, into stories about the experience; instead, we bring our attention to the experience as it happens. And, generally speaking, when we do this we become much more comfortable with the experience.

This helps us to take a calmer, more balanced view in our life. This view is often described as 'equanimity'. Equanimity means neither pushing something away nor dragging it towards you but being okay with staying in the middle. Mindfulness helps us to develop that sense of equanimity by exposing us to experiences and encouraging us to remain present to them.

The same principle applies to most of the activities or experiences that we might feel worried about or that we might be afraid of. If we can go through these experiences mindfully, then gradually we lose the fear or greatly reduce it. In this way, we gain the liberation of being able to go about our business even if we feel a little fearful or nervous.

That is what happens in most cases, but not all. Some actors never lose their stage fright. Some pilots never lose their fear of flying. But day after day, night after night, they face that fear mindfully and pursue successful careers.

All this is not to deny, by the way, that some fears are valuable. The fear of getting knocked down while crossing a road helps to keep us alive. But very often our fears or nervousness don't serve a useful purpose. Generally speaking, we can easily tell which is which. So in practising mindfulness we expose ourselves to our unhelpful fears and in that way we reduce their impact. As a bonus, this increases our tolerance for dealing with issues in our daily lives and expands the range of experiences we can have. That is one of the great gifts of mindfulness and one that is well worth taking advantage of in the future.

As you work with the ideas in this chapter, it's important never to demand that you sail through the situation in a state of total calm. It's okay to be nervous so long as you get things done. What if you're a person who genetically has a higher than average level of reactivity (see 'Getting into your genes: Why de-stressing matters', page 147)? Yes, then you may always find some situations more nerve-inducing than the average person. But that should not mean that you have to avoid situations in your life. Remove the demand that you be completely calm and accept that you will have a residue of nervousness after practising mindfulness. Meanwhile, use the mindfulness exposure method to reduce that nervousness as far as possible. In particular, avoid making matters worse by going into a scenario in your head about these matters.

TRY THESE

Here are some practices that might help you to increase your tolerance for experiences about which you might be nervous or worried.

Practise in nervous situations. When you enter a situation that makes you nervous, try to do so with awareness of your breathing and other physical responses, if it is safe to do so. You could argue that what we are very often afraid of is our own responses rather than the situation itself. This practice will, so to speak, prepare you to be able to tolerate your own feelings when bigger challenges come along. Start with something small. Perhaps you need to make a phone call that makes you nervous – use this as an opportunity for mindful practice.

Practise imaginary exposure. It can also help if you deliberately imagine the situation you are nervous of and again notice your physical reactions. Just imagine yourself in that situation and observe those physical reactions without comment. That 'without comment' is really important. That's how you learn to tolerate your own reactions. Have you ever found that you worried a great deal in advance of an experience and when it happened you sailed through it without bother? You might even have asked yourself what all the worrying was about. All that worry beforehand may well have exposed you to the situation again and again. Your nervousness had, in fact, gone by the time you got around to experiencing it. Of course, this is not a recommendation for worrying, because worrying, after all, is an unpleasant activity, but it is a recommendation to replace excessive worry with mind-fulness practice.

○ QUICK THOUGHT: Use mindful exposure to help you to reduce your level of reactivity to situations that make you feel nervous but that are important to you.

POSITIVE ANXIETY: YES, ANXIETY CAN BE GOOD FOR YOU

Terry is a no-nonsense sort of man. He likes things to work without fuss. So when he came back to a mindfulness workshop, he complained that he had not yet succeeded in getting rid of anxiety. He hoped to achieve that by coming to my workshop again.

I had to inform Terry that we are constructed to experience anxiety as a matter of safety and survival. Mindfulness neither can nor should take away anxiety. What we could hope to do, though, was to change his relationship with anxiety. His aim for the workshop should be to avoid experiencing higher than necessary levels of anxiety.

POSITIVE FEATURES OF ANXIETY

It is important to understand that anxiety also has its positive features.

Instead of immediately saying 'Oh, I must get rid of

this anxiety', you might first ask: 'Does my anxiety have anything helpful to tell me?' And in doing so, remember that anxiety in itself isn't bad for you; it's too much anxiety over too long a period of time that does the harm.

So, in that spirit, here are some positive features of anxiety.

Down and dirty prioritising

Anxiety provides a really quick, down and dirty way of prioritising. Today, we have hundreds of tasks on our to-do lists. Frankly, prioritising all of these tasks properly is beyond us. What anxiety does is to help us prioritise in a rough sort of way. You need to do something about paying that electricity bill, it tells you when you're walking in the park. Or, you'd better ask for help with that project tomorrow morning or it will be too late, it whispers when you'd rather be asleep. It isn't perfect as a reminder system: sometimes anxiety forgets to remind you about things that really matter until it's almost too late. But at least it does some prioritising, and for that we should be grateful. Suppose you're going to a keenly awaited football match tomorrow afternoon. During the night, anxiety taps you on the shoulder to remind you that you promised to have a report on the boss's desk on Monday morning. You may not feel particularly grateful. But as you sit there on

Sunday morning finishing the report, think how much better Monday morning will be thanks to anxiety's prompting.

Anxiety gets you up and going

The shots of adrenalin and cortisol that anxiety gives you makes it hard for you to ignore what it's telling you. Conversely, without those shots you might have found it impossible to summon the energy to get the job done. That's especially so if it is a job that doesn't give you any kind of pleasure. That, at least, is how it is with me and I'm not all that different to the rest of the human race. For instance, if I wasn't anxious about getting my taxes paid on time, I just wouldn't prepare my annual accounts. So anxiety spares me from getting into a no-win situation with the tax people.

Anxiety encourages you to prepare

People who are anxious about public speaking usually give better talks than they thought they would because anxiety made them prepare. Sometimes, the worst talks are given by those who are not anxious at all. So if you're feeling anxious about something – and it doesn't have to be public speaking – take the hint: prepare.

Anxiety makes you address conflicts
you'd rather ignore

Your child is in her school play on Thursday afternoon, but you have been invited to an important meeting at work at the same time. You have decided to go to the meeting. You explain to your child how important the meeting is. You promise to buy her a present for being in the play. But the situation nags at you. It becomes a source of anxiety. If you remain mindful of your anxiety, then you're going to have to do something about it. That might mean talking to your boss or your colleagues about the importance of being with your child on that day. By being mindful, you have improved your chances of making a decision you'll feel good about – and you can put that down to anxiety not allowing you to push the whole dilemma out of your mind.

It's worthwhile acknowledging the role your anxiety plays in helping you to direct your energy in useful ways. It's not just there to scare you. So when you feel the anxiety, pause for a couple of moments to allow into your awareness its potential as a source of energy.

TRY THIS

Here are two ways you can use the helpful aspects of anxiety without getting drowned by those that are simply unhelpful.

Ask yourself, where is the useful anxiety here? Anxiety based on scare stories that you tell yourself and keep recirculating in your head is unlikely to be useful. It's really just a loop in your brain running around and around to no helpful effect. Instead, notice the anxiety and ask yourself, what is useful about this anxiety? Is your anxiety alerting you to something you need to do? Does it make sense to do it? Then why not go ahead and tackle it? But first you might need to . . .

Separate the wheat from the chaff. Chaff is the part of the wheat that is useless for making flour. One of the functions of harvesting machinery is to separate the wheat from the chaff so that only the useful part is left. If you ever saw this being done by an old threshing mill, you will know that a given quantity of wheat can generate a great deal of chaff. Similarly, a given situation can generate a great deal of useless anxiety alongside what's helpful. Asking yourself, as suggested above, where the useful anxiety is can help you to separate the wheat from the chaff.

Not quite convinced . . . : Terry, whom I mentioned at the start, stayed at the workshop and said he would try out what I had said. I think he was still rather dissatisfied that he had not been taught a way to eliminate anxiety completely, but I hope that he succeeded in changing his relationship with anxiety in ways that improved his experience of life.

○ QUICK THOUGHT: Anxiety isn't necessarily bad, and by worrying less and paying more attention to its helpful points, we can be more effective in our day-to-day life.

SITTING QUIETLY, OBSERVE CHANGE

Practice: Sit quietly for a minute or two and notice changes in mind and body but without allowing your attention to be caught by them.

Commentary: Even in such a short time, your thoughts are likely to drift – to something you need to do today or tomorrow or to something that happened yesterday, for instance. You might notice physical changes, too: an itch, a twinge, a tensing and relaxing. By calmly accepting these changes in body and mind, you learn to become less caught up in worries and fears.

Tips: As you go through today, notice changes in your feelings about yourself, the world, the day. You can do this when you are sitting quietly and you can often do it when you are moving about, too. Notice how your thoughts and feelings have changed even over the past half hour. Accept that such changes are the normal pattern of our experience.

COMMON WORRIES

The following twelve worries are representative of issues brought to me by people participating in my mindfulness workshops and courses. In other words, they are common human dilemmas. Mindfulness is an approach employed over thousands of years to help people to relate to their worries in a helpful way. Everybody with any of the issues mentioned here would benefit from engaging in the mindfulness practices outlined in this book, but I have included some specific ideas as well.

1. I SUFFER FROM PANIC ATTACKS.

For the past two years, I have suffered from panic attacks. They can happen anywhere. Usually I feel terrified and sweaty and am afraid of what other people must think of me when I suddenly leave their company. I find that a lot of my time is taken up with my worries that I'm about to have another panic attack.

A great many people have panic attacks – far more than

you might think, because those who suffer from them don't usually talk about it. So having panic attacks doesn't mean there's anything wrong with you. You are not going mad, and I say this because I have come across that hidden fear in a number of people who have panic attacks. By the way, it is almost certain that nobody has actually noticed you having a panic attack – all the unpleasant drama tends to be internal.

If you have not been to see a doctor or spoken to a therapist about your panic attacks, I would recommend you do so. I would also advise you to look at sources of stress in your life and see if you can address these.

Mindfulness suggestion: Learn to observe the onset of a panic attack calmly. By 'calmly', I mean without telling yourself how catastrophic it is that you are having a panic attack. A panic attack can be under way for some time before you actually notice it (see page 111), so the good news is that, by the time you notice it, the attack is on the way to being over.

If you tell yourself how awful it is, or that you must escape, you are in danger of making the panic attack worse. Instead, practise observing the attack as it rises and falls. It will probably have risen and fallen away within 20 minutes or so. Time the length of the attack. Notice how the intensity of the attack changes and also how the symptoms change. You could say to yourself something like: 'This is very unpleasant, but it is already passing.'

Be careful also not to breathe in such a way that you

are gulping air: this can make matters worse because it throws the balance of oxygen and carbon dioxide in your bloodstream out of kilter. So try to breathe as normally as you can.

If you work with these approaches, observing the panic attack as calmly as you can and also breathing as calmly as you can, you will gradually be able to go through panic attacks without having them disrupt your life. This is far better than trying to avoid panic attacks altogether – avoiding them can mean restricting your life more and more as you eliminate places and activities you think are associated with them. Instead, learn to experience panic attacks without needing desperately to get away from them. This brings far greater freedom than desperate avoidance.

As a bonus, you can hope that by following these guidelines you will experience fewer panic attacks, and that they will be shorter and less intense.

2. I AM TERRIFIED OF PUBLIC SPEAKING.

My job means that I often have to speak in public, both to groups of customers and to people in our own office. Although people say that I come across well, I am always terrified at these events and I worry about them for days beforehand. My big fear is that I'm going to forget what I'm saying or that I'm going to show I really don't know what I'm talking about. Just thinking about it makes my throat tighten up and my heart beat faster.

I have heard public speaking described as one of the world's greatest sources of fear! There's something about standing up in front of a group of people and saying your piece that attracts some but terrifies others. And then there's that dread of being 'found out' – of showing that you don't really know what you are talking about. This is a very common, unexpressed fear – I know this as a psychotherapist and because I sometimes experience that fear myself. Even people who have spoken successfully in public many, many times can experience this fear, while knowing that the things they fear are unlikely to happen.

Mindfulness suggestion: When planning a presentation, you need to continually return from thoughts of what might go wrong, which are really just fantasies, and bring your attention back to your planning. If the presentation is already planned and you don't need to do any more work on it, continually bring your attention back to what you are doing right now. That might be going for a walk, or working on another project, or cooking – but whatever it is, practise bringing your attention back to it.

Mindfulness practice can also help during the presentation itself. Before you speak, take a few moments to notice your surroundings, keeping part of your attention on the feeling of your feet against the floor and noticing your breath. That may seem strange, but maintaining a background awareness of your body can bring you a certain stability, a certain presence of mind even in the middle of your presentation.

Notice that we are not trying to arrive at a point at which you will no longer feel nervous about public speaking. We can hope that you will arrive at this point through practice; but first learn to be mindful even when the nervousness is there – that will make a huge difference to your experience both before and during presentations.

3. MY WEEKENDS ARE RUINED BY MONDAY MORNING FEARS.

I used to love my weekends but my job has become increasingly stressful and now I find that I begin to start worrying about Monday morning on Sunday morning. I really feel that this is a big loss to me as I so much value that time with my family. How can I let go of my work worries, at least for the weekend?

If you could bring together all those people who have their Sundays ruined by thoughts of Monday, I reckon you would end up with a very large and gloomy crowd! It's a common experience and one that takes much of the good out of the weekend or whatever your 'off work' days are. The shadow cast by the coming week denies you the rest and recreation you need, and comes between you and your ability to enjoy your weekend activities.

Mindfulness suggestion: First, I would suggest you ensure that you actually have activities planned with your family for the Sunday. Then, whenever your thoughts wander into Monday morning, bring your attention back to your family and to the activity you are engaged in. This may seem a very simple and simplistic exercise, but actually you are training your brain to dwell in the present and not in the future. Over time, you will find it easier and easier to do.

However, it's also reasonable to question whether you should remain in a job that is causing a high level of stress. Of course, all jobs can be stressful on occasion, and you may find this feeling is a passing one, but sometimes we need to question whether we are desperately looking around for strategies to help us 'survive' our work or, indeed, a painful relationship. If we are only 'surviving', changes may be needed.

By encouraging you not to think around and around in circles, mindfulness can help you to see the answers to these questions more clearly. That's because problems are often solved subconsciously, but we need to quieten our minds to allow the answers to come through into awareness. And whatever the answers may be, mindfulness can help you improve your quality of life as you live it.

4. I CAN'T STOP WORRYING ABOUT A MISTAKE I MADE AT WORK.

I made a mistake at work that meant we were late delivering an important order. I don't usually make mistakes but now I find that I am constantly worrying about whether I will, and how these mistakes will make me look in the eyes of my team and my boss. How can I stop worrying about this?

It is natural to feel unease when something like this happens, and to worry about the possible consequences, especially if you are usually efficient. However, if there have been no immediate recriminations arising from this error, it is very unlikely that either your boss or your team are judging you as harshly as you are judging yourself.

Mindfulness suggestion: You need to step away from the scenarios that your mind is generating about making further mistakes – as we all know, the mind is good at conjuring up scary stories. If you want to talk to your boss about what happened, by all means do so. However, it is possible that what is really upsetting you are those scenarios, rather than anything that is likely to actually happen.

Try practising 7/11 breathing (see page 60). This practice gives your mind something more useful to do than dwelling on worries. If you practise this whenever you find yourself reverting to thoughts about this mistake, you will gradually stop giving your mind over to it. (If counting to 11 on the out-breath leaves you gasping, change the numbers: breathe in to a count of 5 and out to a count of 7. The longer out-breath, by the way, is calming.)

You would also find it helpful, when you're at work, to continually bring your attention back to the task you are performing whenever your mind wanders back to your mistake. This way, you are less likely to make another serious mistake and, as a bonus, you will spend less time worrying.

5. I DON'T KNOW HOW I'LL FILL MY DAYS ONCE I RETIRE.

I am due to retire in six months' time. Everybody tells me how wonderful it's going to be but I worry constantly about it. I don't know what I'm going to do with my time and most of my friends are people I work with.

For some, retirement is a long-awaited blessing but for others it is not such a joyful prospect. Unfortunately, everybody is supposed to be jolly about the whole thing, which leaves no room at all for expressing one's fears.

Mindfulness suggestion: In a sense, you are in a 'don't know' space. You know you're retiring but you don't really know what comes afterwards and you're worried about that. So you're filling that space with worry.

Instead, fill the space with present-moment preparations for your impending retirement; perhaps these could include a pre-retirement course. But from a mindfulness point of view, it is not so much the content of the space that is important as your need to deal with your dilemma in the present moment without feeling miserable about a future that has not yet happened. To help with this, continually bring your attention back to the practical aspects of your retirement, but also practise returning to awareness of your breathing. Go for walks, noticing the sights and sounds around you and the feeling of your feet against the ground. This will help to bring you into the present moment in a way that is far more productive than worrying.

6. MY MARRIAGE IS BREAKING UP.

My partner and I have drifted apart over the past few years and lately we have been fighting a lot. Although we have been to marriage counselling, it hasn't helped. I'm very afraid of the future, and I worry about living alone and dealing with all the legal and financial problems that arise after a divorce.

The fears you express are probably of the sort that encourage many people to stay with marriages they would be better off leaving. You are looking at the future right now through an entirely negative lens and that is understandable at this stage of the experience. Mindfulness cannot resolve the practical challenges of a marriage break-up – dealing with legal issues, accommodation and finances, for example – but it can help you to be in the most constructive frame of mind for addressing them. Begin practising mindfulness now to develop it as a resource.

Mindfulness suggestion: Remember some of the principles outlined in the chapter on Morita Therapy (see page 183). Basically, this approach is summed up in three slogans: know your purpose, acknowledge your feelings, and do what needs to be done. So your purpose may be to get through this experience as well as you can; your feelings may be that you're scared; and what needs to be done may be to make a list of steps to take – who you need to consult and what you need to arrange – and then to start working through it. You'll be far better able to do this if you keep bringing your attention back to the task in hand.

It may help also to cultivate the practice of connecting with awareness of your physical sensations. This can be especially useful if you are too distracted to pay attention to your breath. Instead, sit or lie down and become aware of the sensations in your body from your toes to the top of your head. Notice any changes in the sensations. As you do this, breathe as calmly as you can.

Whenever you find yourself caught up in thoughts and fears, give yourself a little break, if you can, to notice these physical sensations. That's always easier than dwelling in a distressed imagination.

7. MY CHILDREN HAVE BECOME SULKY, STROPPY TEENAGERS.

I used to have a good relationship with my children, but lately all they seem to want to do is defy me. I'm now beginning to worry about what we will fight about next, and to dread the moment they return home from school every day and World War Three resumes.

Parents experiencing this problem have lots of company, though it probably doesn't feel that way. This phase is not much fun for teenagers either, especially as they are not yet fully in control of their emotions in terms of brain development. That comes in the early twenties, which probably feels like a long time away for both parent and child.

Mindfulness suggestion: Flashpoints – such as the daily

return from school – are a common feature of teenage rebellion. If you can predict the flashpoints, work mindfully on these. For instance, consider doing some mindful breathing for a short time before your teens come home, so you are in a better frame of mind when they walk through the door.

You might also maintain an awareness of your physical body as you are talking to them. This will help you to remain grounded and not easily swayed by emotion. And if there is a spat between you, a few minutes of mindful walking and bringing your attention to your feet without going around and around the whole argument in your head will help you to calm down.

You may find also that if you are able to remain calm, this may well break the chain of interaction that teenagers are used to. Even when you are firmly standing your ground, if you do so calmly and mindfully there is a good chance that they themselves will become calmer.

The key is to anticipate the flashpoints. Then, instead of talking yourself into an even worse state as it gets closer, use mindfulness techniques to help you arrive at these points, and hopefully get past them, in a calm way.

8. I WORRY ABOUT HOW I'LL PAY THE BILLS.

I am facing financial insecurity and I worry about paying the bills and about my future. I can get by, but I have nothing in reserve for a rainy day. Also, my job is insecure. I worry an awful lot about this and my family have noticed that I am moody and irritable. I find it difficult to sleep.

Financial insecurity is one of those gnawing problems that can take away so much of our peace of mind. It's really important to know how to preserve your strength in the face of such worries and many people have succeeded in doing that even though they still have money problems. Even if some, or maybe most, of your financial problems are outside your control, working on your own peace of mind is within your control.

Mindfulness suggestion: Mindfulness is not going to take your financial insecurity away. What it can do, though, is help you take care of yourself as you deal with whatever issues arise. For instance, mindfulness can help you to get a good night's sleep. As many of us know, it's very easy indeed to lie awake at night worrying about money. The result: exhaustion, with irritability of the kind that affects the whole family.

To get back to sleep, do the body scan described on page 17. It really just involves bringing your awareness back to your body again and again as you move your attention from your feet up to the top of your head. Do this a number of times until you fall asleep. Many people have found the body scan immensely helpful for this purpose. Even if you don't fall asleep, you will be more rested during the coming day.

They say that your health is your wealth but it doesn't

necessarily feel like that when money is very, very tight. Nonetheless, you yourself, ideally with the help of family and friends, can cultivate your emotional and mental wellbeing. Mindfulness, together with other healthy activities, can be of major assistance in doing that. As you work on your own wellbeing, be compassionate towards yourself – in other words, aim to be your own best friend as you navigate your way through the difficult circumstances of financial insecurity.

9. I FEEL INCAPABLE OF JUGGLING WORK AND HOME LIFE.

I spend three hours commuting every day, my job is stressful and my children need my full attention when I get home. Very often I feel like I have nothing left to give and I worry that everything is going to fall apart. I feel completely overwhelmed.

A severe work/life imbalance can certainly make you feel quite trapped and unable to see a way out. You try to do your best in your circumstances but this exacts an exhausting physical and emotional price. However, while you may have very little time for sitting down and putting your feet up, you can take steps to bring some calm into your experience.

Mindfulness suggestion: In this situation, it's useful to practise what I call 'out the door' mindfulness. In other words, you need to be mindful when you're fighting your way out the front door to work while getting the kids off to school, talking to a client on the phone and sticking out a foot to stop the dog escaping. The thought of adding another thing – mindfulness – to such a very busy situation might not be something you want to entertain. But do. You will reap the benefits.

When you find yourself thinking frantically about all you have to do, label those thoughts silently with the word 'thinking' and return to your breathing. Also, make sure you take little breaks during the day, wherever you are. I'm talking about breaks of a minute or so at a time, during which you connect with your breathing and especially the out-breath, which can give you a sense of presence of mind. And before you walk through the door in the evening, pause and take a breath to mark the transition from the workspace to the home space.

These are just three pieces of mindful first aid that might help you to establish a more thoughtful and aware means of going through your day. You might also look at other possible ways to make changes in your life to reduce the demands on you. Meanwhile, adopting the mindfulness practices mentioned here, as well as the others in this book, will help you a very great deal.

10. I FEEL OVERWHELMED WITH GUILT.

I let a friend down and I can't stop worrying about the situation. I failed to defend her when a catty remark was made about her by a group at work. Now I worry that she will find out and despise me for it and I also worry that this means I am not a genuine friend.

Your sense of remorse is very much to your credit. It is clear that you care about your friend and want to do the right thing. Many of us, I fear, have kept silent in a group when we should have defended somebody. Worrying that your friend may find out what happened is an additional stress on top of your feelings about yourself.

Mindfulness suggestion: Allow yourself to experience that sense of regret and remorse but without necessarily going into a storm of thoughts in your head about it. One way to do this is to note the physical sensation of remorse or regret, and allow your attention to rest on the sensation until it changes. Physical sensations always change, whereas thoughts can keep a feeling going for a very long time. Each time the feeling comes back, practise returning to awareness of that physical sensation. In this way, you are not denying your feelings but nor are you recycling the same thoughts endlessly and pointlessly.

11. I WORRY TOO MUCH ABOUT MY CHILDREN.

I worry about my children's future to the point that I'm driving them away. They say that my constant questions and encouragement (as I see it) to do better in their studies so as to get good jobs, and also the fact that I worry about their boyfriends and girlfriends, is so intrusive that as soon as they can they are going to leave home. But I think I'm doing what any parent would do.

Parents always see children as children, even after they have grown up. They, on the other hand, see themselves as the independent adults they are becoming, or that they already are. That being so, parental 'interference' is especially unwelcome from their point of view.

Mindfulness suggestion: When you 'interfere', as the children see it, you are really trying to control the outcome of your children's future in order to rid yourself of your sharp sense of anxiety about it. Instead, when you feel that anxiety, simply acknowledge it, saying silently, 'Yes, I am anxious', and then return to whatever else you are doing right now – a task at work or at home, for example, or going for a walk. Returning your attention to your activity does not negate your concern for your children. You know you would do anything for them. But you don't need to keep reminding yourself or them of this fact. What you need instead is to be able to relate differently to your own anxiety so that it doesn't destroy your relationship with your children.

12. I FEAR FOR MY HEALTH.

I've been ill and now I can't stop worrying that I'm going to get ill again. I had never been ill before, beyond having a cold or flu, and it actually came as a shock to me when I had to go to hospital. It wasn't a very serious illness but now I know I'm just as vulnerable as anybody else I find it plays on my mind that I may not be able to do what I need to for my family, or for my business. I have been told to 'live in the now' but that is much easier said than done.

Illness comes as quite a shock to those of us who go around imagining that it's something that happens to other people. What's happening now is that the realisation of something that was always true – namely, that you are as vulnerable as the next person – has struck you full force.

Mindfulness suggestion: What you need to do from a mindfulness point of view is to respect the fact that you have this fear, and recognise that it probably came out of that realisation of vulnerability that the illness brought on. Allow yourself to feel the fear, but without catastrophising – in other words, without building a series of scary scenarios in your head: *If I get sick will I lose my business and then my home and then my family?* That sort of thing.

The aim of using mindfulness isn't so much to take away the fear of being ill as to drop these exaggerated imaginings, which only make things worse. So practise noticing the fear and then returning your attention calmly to awareness of your breathing, or of walking or working. You might have to acknowledge it one hundred times before you notice a difference but gradually, because mindfulness makes you less reactive to negative thoughts, you should find that the fear itself becomes less and less.

You can also practise acceptance by acknowledging

that, yes, like every other human being I am vulnerable to illness. I will not seek to make myself invulnerable and I will not seek to drive my fear away. I accept my vulnerability and my fear and then I get on with my life.

RESOURCES

The most important resource is your own practice of the techniques you have read about in this book. However, the extra resources listed here, which are low-cost or free, will help you to broaden (by learning further methods) and deepen (by encouraging you to practise more) your experience and use of mindfulness. They will help you to bring mindfulness to your relationship with worry, anxiety and stress and thereby enhance your quality of life.

In addition to these resources, you are very welcome to email me at any time at pomorain@gmx.com

BOOKS

Mindfulness on the Go: Peace in Your Pocket (Padraig O'Morain)
Written to provide all the elements of mindfulness to people in a hurry in today's world.

Light Mind: Mindfulness for Daily Living (Padraig O'Morain)
A comprehensive introduction to mindfulness and its application.

Calming Your Anxious Mind (Jeffrey Brantley MD)
A blend of mindfulness and Western psychology aimed at people suffering anxiety.

The Happiness Trap (Russ Harris)
A practical and engaging book on Acceptance and Commitment Therapy, which explains mindfulness in easily understood and memorable ways.

Don't Sweat the Small Stuff . . . and it's all Small Stuff (Richard Carlson)
This hugely popular book and the 'Small Stuff' series is based solidly on Buddhist and mindfulness principles.

Wherever You Go, There You Are (Jon Kabat-Zinn)
Dip into the brief readings on mindfulness in this book by arguably the major figure in the mindfulness movement in the past thirty years.

Full Catastrophe Living (Jon Kabat-Zinn)
This major book by Kabat-Zinn is based on his ground-breaking work on mindfulness for people with chronic pain and chronic stress.

Mindfulness: Finding peace in a frantic world (Prof Mark Williams and Dr Danny Penman)
Prof Williams is one of the world's leading authorities on mindfulness for depression and anxiety.

Sane New World: Taming the Mind (Ruby Wax)
Partly a psychological biography and partly an explanation of mindfulness, this book offers a blend of humour and learning.

WEBSITES

www.padraigomorain.com
My website has many free mindfulness resources, including audios relevant to this book.

www.todoinstitute.org
The ToDo Institute has been bringing Japanese, mindfulness-based approaches to the West for decades. They include approaches such as Morita Therapy and Naikan, mentioned in this book.

www.everyday-mindfulness.org
Everyday Mindfulness has many articles on applying mindfulness to your everyday life.

www.freemindfulness.org
Lots of free audios (including some by myself) and other

resources on this great website from the Free Mindfulness Project.

www.wildmind.org
The Wildmind Buddhist website features good online courses, a good blog and lots of interesting articles.

NEWSLETTERS

(Subscribe at www.padraigomorain.com)

The Daily Bell
Thousands of people all over the world receive my free daily mindfulness email. Many say it provides an invaluable aid to their mindfulness practice.

Padraig O'Morain's Mindfulness Newsletter
This free newsletter, issued by email every two to three weeks, includes brief articles on mindfulness, as well as quotes and links to resources.

COURSES

I present a variety of mindfulness courses in Ireland and the UK. To keep in touch with what's on where and when, subscribe to my newsletter (above) or to my Daily Bell daily mindfulness reminder or visit the website.

Online: Check out my online mindfulness course, Mindfulness Without Meditation, at www.padraigomorain.com.

YOUTUBE

A YouTube search for 'Mark Williams' and 'Jon Kabat-Zinn' will reveal many very helpful videos featuring these world-leading mindfulness teachers and researchers.

INSIGHT TIMER

A popular and useful app for iPhone, iPad and Android.

AUDIO

You will find free audio related to this book on my website: www.padraigomorain.com

ACKNOWLEDGEMENTS

I am grateful to my publisher, Liz Gough of Yellow Kite Books, to my agent, Susan Feldstein of The Feldstein Agency, and to my editor, Jayne Ansell, who have ushered this book onto the shelves and into your hands.

INDEX

feet, awareness of 108, 116, 120, 205

fight or flight 154

fighting, and relationships 165–71

financial worries 212–14

5 per cent rule 180–1

flashpoints 211–12

floor, breathing through the 164

form the intention practice 54

future, fear of the 2

G

generalised anxiety disorder (GAD) 107, 108–9

genes
  genetic inheritance 159–63
  and stress 147–51

get up and go 197

give 5 per cent practice 24

Glasser, Dr William 102

glucocorticoids 2, 57

guilt 215–16

H

habituation 140–1

hands, awareness practice 84

health 213–14
  worries about 217–19

holding on to attachments 101–5

home life, juggling with work 214–15

'how does this help me' practice 67

I

illness, worries about 217–19

imaginary worries 39–43

immune system 56

imperfections 65–6, 129

impermanence 136–42

impressing people 46–7

inherited anxiety 158–63

insomnia 213

insula 150

intentions, forming mindful 54

J

juggling work and home life 214–15

'just worrying' practice 36–7, 83

L

labelling experiences 115

lake, calming the 38

listening 74

locking in to worries 76–9

loving kindness practice 173–4